Threatened Landscapes

Threatened Landscapes

Conserving cultural environments

Edited by Bryn Green and Willem Vos

London and New York

333.72
T531

First published 2001
by Spon Press
11 New Fetter Lane, London EC4P 4EE

Simultaneously published in the USA and Canada
by Spon Press
29 West 35th Street, New York, NY 10001

Spon Press is an imprint of the Taylor & Francis Group

© 2001 selection and editorial matter: Bryn Green and Willem Vos;
individual chapters: the contributors

The right of Bryn Green and Willem Vos and the contributors to
be identified as the Authors of this Work has been asserted by them
in accordance with the Copyright, Designs and Patents Act 1988

Typeset in Frutiger by Keystroke, Jacaranda Lodge, Wolverhampton
Printed and bound in Great Britain by Bell and Bain Ltd, Glasgow

All rights reserved. No part of this book may be reprinted or
reproduced or utilised in any form or by any electronic, mechanical,
or other means, now known or hereafter invented, including
photocopying and recording, or in any information storage or
retrieval system, without permission in writing from the publishers.

The publisher makes no representation, express or implied, with
regard to the accuracy of the information contained in this book
and cannot accept any legal responsibility or liability for any errors
or omissions that may be made.

British Library Cataloguing in Publication Data
A catalogue record for this book is available from the British Library

Library of Congress Cataloging in Publication Data
Threatened landscapes: conserving cultural environments/edited by
Bryn Green and Willem Vos.
    p. cm.
  Includes bibliographical references.
  1. Landscape protection 2. Nature conservation. I. Green, Bryn.
  II. Vos, W. (Willem)
QH75 .T47 2001
333.7′2–dc21   00–069823

ISBN 0–419–25630–X

Contents

University Libraries
Carnegie Mellon University
Pittsburgh, PA 15213-3890

Contents

Foreword

The concept of landscape locks people and their activities firmly into conservation planning and management. Landscape conservation is an accepted and well-established component of conservation strategies in Europe, but much less accepted elsewhere. I attended a number of meetings of the Landscape Conservation Working Group, where its members gave freely and enthusiastically of their time to promote the development of landscape conservation to which they are all committed. My experience around the world as a CESP Chairman led me to the conviction that Landscape Conservation is an important tool for sustainability which is applicable in many parts of the world. The promotion of such practical means of achieving conservation objectives was a major plank in CESP activity during my time and I urge its continued promotion, confident in its relevance, effectiveness and success.

Ted Trzyna
Former Chairman IUCN/CESP

Preface

It is increasingly realized that few, if any, environments are free of human intervention and, moreover, that in many environments such intervention is a key element in generating and maintaining biodiversity. In many parts of the world human intervention has created and maintained environments which are arguably richer and more diverse in species, scenic beauty, historical interest and recreational opportunity than the natural forest and other ecosystems they have replaced. These environments, ranging from the mixed farm and forestlands of Europe and eastern North America, through the pasture lands and savannahs of the Middle East and Africa to the paddylands of the Pacific Rim, are usually the product of relatively low-level, sustainable exploitation of the environment over long periods of time. They are commonly called cultural landscapes.

Although many such areas are protected by various designations, in other parts of the world general recognition and acceptance of the concept of landscape conservation has been slow. Even when accepted, the conservation of entire cultural landscapes often presents great practical difficulties. Everywhere they are threatened by changes in agriculture, demography, urbanization and other transformations of old rural economies.

New impetus has been given to the conservation of threatened landscapes by the rapid development of the new discipline of landscape ecology. It was through the initiative of a pioneer in this discipline, Zev Naveh, that the International Association of Landscape Ecologists (IALE) and the World Conservation Union (formerly known as IUCN) came to establish the Landscape Conservation Working Group (LCWG) as part of the IUCN Commission on Environmental Strategy and Planning (CESP). Resolution 19.40 of the General Assembly at Buenos Aires in 1994 mandated the work of the group, in particular asking for a pilot study of threatened landscapes.

This book is an elaboration of that study, written by members of the Working Group and others who contributed to it. Many other people have made substantial contributions to the work in different ways. Yoav Sagi promoted the adoption of Resolution 19.40 and played a key role in developing landscape-listing concepts and methodologies. Almo Farina organized the conference where the first workshop meeting of the LCWG took place and maintained links with IALE. CESP Former Chairman Ted Trzyna was an active and enthusiastic supporter of the Group. Inez Woltjer and Jean Green have made substantial and invaluable editorial contributions. We are most grateful to them all.

Bryn Green and Willem Vos

Contributors

Fred. Aalen, Department of Geography, Trinity College, Dublin 2, Ireland

Ingrid Austad and Leif Hauge, Department of Landscape Ecology, Sogn og Fjordane College, Box 133, N-6801 Sogndal, Norway

Diedrich Bruns, Universität Gesamthochschule Kassel, Nordbahnhofstr. 1a, DE-37213 Witzenhausen, Germany

Bob Bunce, Centre for Ecology and Hydrology, Merlewood Research Station, Grange-over-Sands, Cumbria LA11 6JU, UK

Chen Changdu, Department of Geography, University of Beijing, Beijing 100871, China

Bryn Green, 16B The Granville, Hotel Road, St. Margaret's Bay, Dover, Kent, CT15 6DX, UK

Henk Greven, Institute for Forestry and Nature Research (IBN-DLO), PO Box 23, NL-6700 AA, Wageningen, The Netherlands

Dick Grove, Jennifer Moody and Oliver Rackham, Department of Geography, University of Cambridge, Downing Place, Cambridge, CB2 3EN, UK

Ioannis Ispikondis and Vasilios Papanastasis, Laboratory of Range Science, University of Thessaloniki, 54006 Thessaloniki, Greece

Peter Kaland, Department of Geography, University of Bergen, Breiviksveien 40, N-5045 Bergen, Norway

Didi Kaplan, Nature Reserves Authority, Safed, Israel 13111

Ladislav Miklos, Institute of Landscape Ecology, Slovak Academy of Sciences, Stefanikova 3, 81499 Bratislava, Slovak Republic

Miguel Morey, Departament de Biologia Ambiental, Universitat de les Illes Balears, 07071 Palma de Majorca, Spain

Teresa Pinto-Correia and José Mascarenhas, Department of Ecology, Universidad Evora, 7001 Evora Cedex, Portugal

Gloria Pungetti, Department of Geography, University of Cambridge, Downing Place, Cambridge, CB2 3EN, UK

Jim Russell, Centre for Environmental Studies, University of Tasmania, Hobart 7001, Tasmania, Australia.

Toshinori Shigematsu, Kyushu Institute of Design, Fukuoka 815, Japan

Eunice Simmons, P.H. Huxley School, Imperial College at Wye, University of London, Wye, Kent TN25 5AH, UK

Dirk Wascher, European Centre for Nature Conservation, PO Box 1352, NL-5004 BJ, Tilburg, The Netherlands

Willem Vos, Institute for Forestry and Nature Research (IBN-DLO), PO Box 23, NL-6700 AA, Wageningen, The Netherlands

Yoshiro Yamamori, Kyoritsu Women's Junior College, Tokyo 101, Japan.

Part One

What are landscapes?

Chapter 1

Landscape development and change

F.H.A. Aalen

> We do not enough conceive for ourselves that variegated mosaic of the world's surface which a bird sees in its migration . . . We know the differences in detail, but we have not that broad glance and grasp which would enable us to feel them in their fulness.
>
> (Ruskin, J. 1844)

Introduction

The great physical and cultural variety of Europe has resulted in a profusion of contrasting landscapes. Broad latitudinal zones of distinctive relief, climate and natural vegetation cross the continent; moving from south to north, they include the Mediterranean evergreen woodland, the massive barrier of Alpine ranges, a wide belt of temperate deciduous forest on the North European Plain and, beyond it, the subarctic coniferous forest and treeless tundra of the Scandinavian north. Within these major ecozones, and especially marked in the major mountain chains, there is a mosaic of interlinked local ecologies. This ecological frame has actively influenced a long, eventful history involving many ethnic groups and major civilizing forces. A complex pattern of agrarian settlement traditions emerged, intimately adjusted to the natural background but also transforming it. European landscapes are indeed a complex meshing of nature and culture, created by millennia of dynamic interaction between communities and their habitats. Through the careful study and historical reconstruction of these landscapes we can uncover new and useful evidence of humanity's transformation of and by the earth.

The study of landscape history

Landscape history aims to describe and understand landscapes in their entirety (embracing all features be they contemporary, historic, abandoned or buried) and as objectively as possible, and to construct a realistic account of the long-term processes of landscape development using fieldwork, aerial survey, relevant scientific techniques and historical sources. As an object of study, the landscape is shared by many disciplines. It is central to landscape ecology and has been a long-standing if fluctuating concern within geography. Other contributing disciplines include: palaeoecology, which provides detailed accounts of past vegetation and landscape change and is especially relevant to the earliest and inescapably obscure phases of human transformation of nature which have left few or no traces in the present landscape (Birks *et al*. 1988); landscape archaeology, which attempts to reconstruct the totality of settlement patterns in ancient landscapes (Fleming 1998, Fabech & Ringtved 1999, Ucko & Layton 1999, Cooney 2000); and environmental history, or ecohistory, a strengthening historical field embracing an ecological perspective on human activities as against the perceived 'anthropocentricity' of traditional history and much of geography (Worster 1988, Russell 1997, Grove & Rackham 2001).

Landscape history is thus inherently inter-disciplinary and without an agreed body of theory or methodology. However, it is a potentially strong medium for unifying the varied perceptions of the complex aspects of landscape and thereby generating some rapprochement between disparate and discrete bodies of knowledge. Society and its environment are in constant transition, and understanding their inter-connections in the formation of a landscape requires collaboration between humanities and sciences and deep time-perspectives. *La longue durée* is also essential to effective landscape management; carefully locating the present in a long-term trajectory of change highlights the historical and ecological significance of the landscape's present-day components and helps to evaluate the potential impact of contemporary and future trends.

There is at present an upsurge of interest in landscape study in several disciplines. In part, this reflects attempts to overcome perceived deficiencies of approach within the disciplines themselves. However, it is also a mani-festation of wider public awareness that landscapes are rapidly changing and that their quality and diversity have been seriously diminished in recent decades by many potent forces, such as intensive mechanized farming, large-scale afforestation, mass tourism, despoliation around industrial cities and the abandonment and decay of valued cultural landscapes owing to rural de-population. Peoples and governments, it is now argued, must protect and enhance landscape qualities, and the landscape has moved on to international as well as national policy agendas (Stanners & Bourdeau 1995, Aalen *et al*. 1997). At the same time, landscape approaches have moved into the mainstreams of conservation thought, mainly through the agency of landscape ecology. The idea of landscape has singular applicability to current problems and policies. To 'think landscape' is to think not about single elements but about wholes which are expressions of coherent natural and cultural pro-cesses. This focus on the linkage of nature and people has a special resonance in the post-Rio period with landscapes presented as natural frameworks for initiatives in sustainable development (Wascher 2000).

The meshing of nature and culture

Research in various disciplines over recent decades has provided evidence that human influences on nature are more pervasive and profound than formerly envisaged and has brought a fuller appreciation of the deep historical roots of Europe's landscapes. Vegetation types and soil types, for example, have been much modified by prehistoric and historic systems of land use, and many landscape elements once regarded as natural, such as grasslands, bogs, heaths and karsts, have been deeply influenced by humans. Save in the remoter parts of the northern taiga forests, little survives of the continent's natural primary forest cover, owing to clearance and disturbance by the grazing, burning and woodcutting activities of farming communities. The depleted forests, however, have been decisive in shaping the prevailing patterns of secondary vegetation. In long settled and deeply humanized areas such as Europe, a simple distinction between natural and cultural landscapes is thus unwarranted; the concept of a gradient of human impact is more useful (Birks *et al.* 1988).

The close intertwining of human and natural processes complicates the reconstruction of landscape history. Hence, it is often difficult, especially in prehistory, to disentangle natural from human processes and establish a clear pattern of causation. It is not always clear, for example, whether or how far the patterns observable in a fossil pollen record are the result of climatic changes or human impacts; early deforestation by humans may alter vegetation in ways that mimic climatic shifts, and at some stages humans may have been accentuating natural changes, while in others working contrary to them. Or again, did the frequent submergence of prehistoric fields and settlements under peat bogs in Britain and Ireland result simply from natural processes of bog expansion during moist phases, or was it induced by early human interference with the natural vegetation cover, leading to intensified leaching, hard-pan development and local waterlogging? Even more controversial is the interpretation of Greek environmental history. The stony barrenness of much of Greece seems incongruous with the great cultural achievements in the Bronze Age and classical times. Was the land greener and more productive during the great days of Greek civilization and was it the demands of civilization which eventually precipitated an environmental collapse through deforestation, soil erosion and overgrazing? Or could environmental changes without human agency have led to the cultural decline? Yet another possibility is that the Greek environment has not substantially changed at all and cultural eminence and decline resulted from purely social and political processes. Despite considerable recent research on Greece, there are still widely divergent views on these matters (Rackham 1990, Runnels 1995), although the weight of expert opinion seems to lie with anthropic origins and point to a long history of misusing the land.

Changes in cultural landscape are expressed not only in human settlement patterns and the rural economy but have often involved considerable alteration to the physical setting by, for example, drainage, flood control, and modification and erosion of the soil. Contemporary landscape in many places has been so deeply modified by human activity that it can be a misleading analytical template upon which to base studies of past human settlement and exploitation; earlier settings, especially on flood plains and the surroundings of major cities, must be carefully reconstructed using a variety of methods. Most societies have had to relate to already deeply humanized landscapes, not to a natural environment, and while it is an exaggeration to speak of 'retrospective determinisms', such landscapes are not simply a passive recipient of human activity but an active element in the evolution of the society using it, constraining and influencing the activities of subsequent inhabitants (Chapman & Dolukhanov 1997).

Time layers in the landscape

Aerial survey, field archaeology and improved geochronological techniques have shown that prehistoric populations in Europe were more numerous and their settlements and field systems more widespread and ordered than once assumed (Cunliffe 1994). Moreover, many of the cultural outlines in the present-day landscape are much older than previously thought. For example, regular land divisions still visible on the infields in southern Vastergotland (Sweden) seem to be prehistoric in origin, and walled enclosures associated with Iron Age forest clearances on the Baltic island of Gotland have survived into historic times (Helmfrid 1994). On Dartmoor and in other areas of England, there are extensive fossil field systems consisting of long, parallel stony banks (reaves), often extending for many miles, which are attributed to large-scale landscape planning in the Bronze Age (Rackham 1986). Comparable field patterns of Neolithic date have been discovered under bogs in western Ireland and the excavated dry-stone walls are similar to and, in some instances, connect with the walls still used on the surrounding land (Cooney 2000).

Some ancient agrarian structures have been notably enduring. For example, centuriation, a regular grid of rectangular holdings with an approximate area of 50 ha, originated as part of a systematic general plan for colonization in parts of the Roman Empire. Many later features were inserted, but the imprint of these monumental frameworks can still be clearly seen in many areas, such as the Po plains and Campania (Italy), and the basic lines often determine the orientation of fields and lines of trees as well as boundaries and local roads (Sereni 1997). Rectilinear field systems were used earlier in planned Greek colonies and can still be traced in the landscapes of the Mediterranean and Black Sea coasts. These extensive Roman and Greek projects are somewhat comparable in their scale and endurance to the archetypal dry-field (ti) landscapes of the North China plain; the latter are characterized by narrow, rectangular plots which, it has been suggested, may represent a progressive subdivision of an earlier chequerboard pattern, introduced by the state to distribute land to peasants in equal units.

Clearly, present-day landscapes are not the product of modern activities alone but have matured over lengthy periods of prehistoric and historic time and bear the imprint of a range of past cultures and patterns of land use and settlement. Indeed, at every point in history a landscape always consists largely of its past. A sequence, or palimpsest, of distinctive landscape patterns is sometimes discernible, superimposed on each other. Each time the landscape was remodelled, fragments of the earlier system tended to survive in undisturbed places or to show through the newer pattern in a subdued, less legible form. These earlier patterns can be readily distinguished when they are independent features out of phase with standing field divisions and roads. Where, however, older features, such as field boundaries, have been adapted and incorporated piecemeal into a changing landscape, they may be difficult to identify without careful study and the antiquity and continuity of landscape features can consequently be underestimated. Extensive traces of early landscapes remain buried beneath the ground surface and can be revealed with uncanny clarity on aerial photographs as 'crop-marks', subtle colour variations in crops growing above the sub-surface archaeological remains. Photographs taken in contrasting weather and crop conditions provide extra detail and permit a composite map of the 'hidden landscape'; this is particularly helpful in fertile, arable areas where earlier surface features have often been erased by successive occupation and intensive cultivation.

Dynamics of landscape change

The dialectic between society and habitat leads to a continuous process of landscape change. Cultural changes, such as population increase, growing social complexity and technological capacities, constantly alter human relationships to their environment. The environment itself can sometimes change independently through, for example, climatic change, shifts in sea level or the spread of plant and animal diseases, but landscape changes are more often a direct response to human impacts. Although phases of marked landscape transformation through human agency can be recognized, change was normally gradual and partial because the ability to restructure human ecology developed slowly and the inherited landscape fabric, so costly of human effort to create, remained intact unless subjected to exceptional pressures. Even in the most artificial landscapes, however, human activities do not override ecological processes. Rather they channel them towards a culturally preferred outcome, which may not be stable or sustainable in the long run. It seems that land-use practices have often been continued to the verge of ecological breakdown and the succession of fundamental trans-formations evident in the history of cultural landscapes, whilst no doubt multi-causal, may in part reflect the search for new relationships with nature made necessary by the instability or failure of earlier ones. The landscape palimpsests of Europe are expressions of changing socio-economic organization, but the crucial question is how far the changes were of necessity or choice. Palimpsests also reflect the resilience of European nature, which, in a relatively benign climate, had the capacity to absorb change and regenerate, its recuperative powers generally outbalancing various forms of misuse.

The idea that the land-use systems of pre-agricultural and traditional peasant societies were relatively stable owing to practices and beliefs evolved to maintain some equilibrium with the landscape and involving concepts of resource conservation has support among some ethno-ecologists but may be misguided (Sanders & Webster 1994). Human adaptation is highly dynamic and population growth and societal changes were invariably accompanied by

1.1 Landscape palimpsest, Swaledale, North Yorkshire, England

Swaledale is characterized by the classic landscape features of the Pennine dales; dispersed family farms, striking patterns of walled fields producing grass and hay for sheep and cattle, and scattered hay barns roofed and walled with stone and attached to the field walls. Essentially formed some three to four hundred years ago, this pastoral landscape provided a dramatic change from that of the later Middle Ages when population expansion had led to heavy cultivation. Many traces of the medieval agrarian pattern survive, including deserted and shrunken settlements and strip lynchets (man-made cultivation terraces) which are often arranged in distinct groups and provided a means of conserving the light soils exposed to heavy rainfall on the steep dale-sides. There are also traces of Iron Age and Romano-British landscape features, such as earthworks, field banks and settlement platforms. The photograph illustrates the intricacy within a small tract of landscape. The wall running between A and A is on an early post-Roman linear earthwork, one of the Grinton – Fremington dykes. To the right of B is a probable Romano-British settlement, and there is another of uncertain age between C and D. Also visible are the fragmentary banks of an Iron Age/Romano-British field system, and traces of medieval and post-medieval ploughing and terracing. (Photograph: Andrew Fleming) an intensified use of the natural environment which was opportunistic and little concerned with long-range problems. There was a tendency to stretch practices to their limits where unpredictable set-backs could easily precipitate ecological collapse. It seems likely that industrial societies differ from pre-industrial chiefly in their enhanced ability to destroy the environment and not in any basic change in approach to long-term problems. Farmers in all ages have caused erosion and impoverishment of the soil and irreparable environmental damage to many areas. But they have also established relatively sustainable land-use systems and landscapes. Both the successes and the failures merit close study and comparison.

How ecological dynamics were incorporated and woven into earlier patterns of everyday social practice is the key concern in our attempts to reconstruct landscape history and to understand the ecological significance of present-day landscape features, most of which are a legacy from past centuries. Contemporary trends, such as urbanization, industrialization, intensive scientific farming and improved communications are leading to cultural stan-dardization and a growing degree of landscape homogenization, but the use of local resources is still in many places determined by cultural and landscape heritage rooted in the distant past. The perspective of landscape ecology, especially if it is given a deep and fully informed time dimension, is particularly helpful to landscape management, the past being necessary not only to understand the present but to evaluate the outcome of modern trends and the impacts of future policy proposals, especially those aiming to bring about the transition to sustainable land-use patterns. Purposeful change must be based on true understanding of the natural and human processes which determine the nature of places.

Prehistoric outlines

The numerous mesolithic foraging communities of Europe may have made local modifications to their forested environments, especially through the burning of natural vegetation to encourage young shoots and to attract deer. However, it was farmers, with their intimate and sustained relation to the land over thousands of years, who were the dominant agents of landscape change and continuity; their major achievement being the large-scale clearance of the natural forest cover and its replacement with a distinctive agrarian landscape of farms and fields, infinitely varied in character by sensitive local adaptations to the cleared terrain and progressive environmental transformation through drainage, terracing, fertilizing and other means of soil enhancement. Deforestation, however, was a slow and uneven process with successive phases of clearance and regrowth. Moreover, forests have remained important elements in the landscape, surviving best on the sunless slopes of major mountain ranges unattractive to farming, and much changed by grazing, cutting and burning. Today, forests cover close to 30 per cent of Europe, although varying considerably between countries; without human interference, over 80 per cent would be covered by forests.

Archaeological and other evidence indicates that farming was introduced into prehistoric Europe from south-west Asia. Small farming communities had

1.2 Veruela, near Tarazona, Aragon, Spain

In the bottom of the valley (centre left in the picture) is the 12th century Cistercian monastery of Veruela surrounded by well-organized cultivated land and plantations. The fringing uplands remain generally uncultivated and bare. From the 11th century onwards, the highly disciplined monastic orders, especially the Cistercian order founded in 1098, were major pioneers in land reclamation and agricultural innovation and in the application of mechanical devices and sources of energy, which allowed the monks to economize their labour and give time to religious duties. With well over 300 foundations in the 12th century, Cistercian enterprise has had an enduring influence on the landscapes of many parts of Europe from Scandinavia to the Mediterranean basin. (Photograph: Timothy Darvill) penetrated the Balkans by the seventh millennium BC, seeking out well-watered cultivable localities, such as lake and river shores and inactive levees on floodplains, in order to survive the summer drought. Thereafter, following a course finely tuned to ecological and cultural variations, it took some 3000 years for farming to spread along the Mediterranean basin and over the continent to the climatic limits of crop production in southern Scandinavia (Harris 1996). In order to flourish on the North European Plain farmers had to make effective adaptations to the problems of winter cold and fodder shortages through techniques such as hay-making and stall-feeding. The earliest farmers north of the Alps appear to have been immigrant communities with distinctive pottery (LBK) and long-houses who spread over the forested loess and other areas of light soils in central Europe. Along the agricultural frontiers, it seems that the aboriginal mesolithic communities progressively adopted neolithic elements into their cultures; some indeed may have been incipient cultivators already using techniques such as burning, weeding and elementary irrigation. The successful, more sedentary foraging groups in the circum-Baltic region on the northern fringe of the Plain long resisted displacement or assimilation, presumably because they had little immediate use for domesticates, and only population pressure and loss of territory owing to the Litorina submergence led to their adoption of agricultural economies. In general, however, European foragers became farmers, and over the continent as a whole it is likely that neolithic cultures were deeply indebted to mesolithic environmental knowledge and skills.

Pastoral nomadism developed from mixed farming in marginal areas of the Old World where cultivation was precarious but animals could flourish. Nomads became well adapted to arid environments and, with the domestication of the horse and camel, highly mobile and skilled in warfare. This allowed them to expand widely on the Eurasian steppes, often displacing farmers who had colonized the moister fringes of the grasslands where the rainfall, although irregular, was just sufficient for grain crops. The boundaries between nomad and peasant were often unstable and depended on the local balance of power. From the third millennium BC, there were successive waves of nomad expansion from the western parts of the steppe into Europe, sometimes deflected northwards around the Carpathians to the plains of northern Europe but impinging mainly on the South East and resulting in the removal of peasantry and the spread of grassland; the most recent incursion was the Magyar invasion of the Hungarian Plain at the end of the ninth century AD. The well-developed and long-surviving regimes of transhumant pastoralism in south-eastern Europe may reflect some fusion of peasant and nomadic societies.

Historic landscapes

There has been substantial continuity of landscape patterns and settlement forms from the Middle Ages. Over most of Europe until the seventeenth and eighteenth centuries, nucleated villages prevailed in association with complex modes of communally controlled resource management, allowing each farmer access to the varied resources of the village territory but also linking together

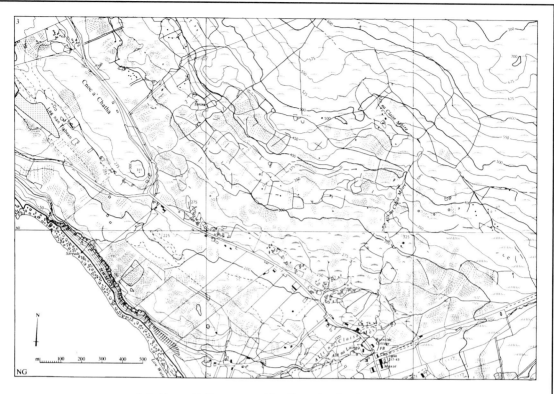

1.3 Upper Halistra township, Skye, Scotland

The remains of an extensive 18th century crofting township are here strung along a coastal road; they include a variety of buildings and associated yards, together with field walls, rig cultivation and cairns, forming a complete historic landscape. Relatively recently abandoned settlements like this occur across much of Scotland, remarkable in their quality, extent and completeness. Crofting townships comprised small, compact, tenant holdings often with access to common grazing and fishing resources. They originated in the rural upheavals of the 18th and 19th centuries associated with population pressures and the Improvement Movement. Many were derived from the reorganization of older clustered settlements (touns) and run-rig cultivation: the transformation was normally thoroughgoing, but evidence of the earlier order, especially the nuclear areas of settlement, is sometimes discernible in the reformed landscape. Run-rig itself may have gradually spread over an earlier pattern of irregular enclosures, perhaps prehistoric in origin, fragments of which also survive. This succession of changes, terminating in large-scale modern depopulation, is an eloquent reminder of the instability which has characterized the landscapes of many upland and climatically marginal areas. (Photograph: Royal Commission on the Ancient and Historical Monuments of Scotland)

and conserving them. Through multiple use and wide spatial linkages it was possible to exploit rural resources more comprehensively, though less intensively, than does modern specialized, mechanized and scientific farming. The broad spectrum of uses gave traditional landscapes much of their distinctive character as well as some stability (Pfeiffer 1956, Pounds 1979).

An efficient interlocking of cultivation and livestock was crucial to the old village economy. The arable land surrounding the villages was generally worked on the open-field system with the holdings of individual farmers distributed in numerous, scattered, unenclosed plots. Livestock grazed on commonages at a distance from the village. Each year, after harvesting, the village livestock were turned loose on the arable area to help restore its fertility. In addition, the arable plots were aggregated into large portions or 'fields' which could be successively fallowed (ploughed but not sown) for a period of years. Two-field systems were found in various scattered parts of Europe and were dominant throughout the Mediterranean and in Poland. The more advanced three-field system was best developed on productive lowland soils north of the Alps. It was associated with a strong emphasis on cereal growth, but small animal populations and limited manure hindered productivity. Hill areas and heaths (developed often on lowland patches of sandy glacial outwash), although forming islands of infertility, were consequently much valued for grazing, and damp stretches near streams were used for hay-making.

The use of fallowing continued on the open fields down to the modern introduction of intensification methods such as crop rotations and reclamation of marshlands for livestock grazing. From the late eighteenth century and through the nineteenth century, as the ideas of agricultural improvement spread, there was a tendency for communal agrarian organization on open fields to be replaced by independent, consolidated holdings, a development evident in Denmark, the Hungarian Plain and southern Italy, for example. However, the process of reform was often incomplete and new features clearly owe much to earlier systems; for example, the old patterns and characteristic curvature of medieval strips have left a strong imprint on the new reformed fieldscapes, especially in the consolidated but unenclosed farmlands such as the Paris Basin, and they are often reflected too in areas where new fields were enclosed by hedges and walls.

The temperate forests, most often deciduous or mixed with conifers, were generally managed and preserved as an integral part of the old village economy, providing, among other things, pasturage for swine and cattle, fodder, litter for stalls, game and edible berries and plants, timber for domestic and industrial buildings, and fuel. The penetration of forests for pasturing was sometimes a prelude to permanent clearing for agriculture and settlement. Assarting, the piecemeal encroachment of farmlands on the forests and heaths, was characteristic of periods of rising population. But the boundaries of farmland, forest and moorland were constantly fluctuating in response not only to population trends but also market trends, technological changes, political instability, warfare and population displacement. Abandoned farmland was often recolonized by the forest. In north-western Europe, however, after the extensive prehistoric clearances, the forests seem never to have regained their former dominance, giving way to rough pasture and blanket bogs used chiefly by transhumant herders; woodland regeneration, however weak, was constantly checked by grazing and burning. Periodic expansion and contraction of settlement in these marginal areas is clearly marked by plentiful remnants of cultivation, including walls and fossil plough ridges.

In the deeply humanized, sub-tropical Mediterranean zone, the natural cover of evergreen woodland, never so dense as the forests of temperate Europe, has been depleted in a variety of ways and for many purposes. Where complete clearance has taken place for cultivation or pasture, the landscapes are now typified by distinctive associations of crops and plants such as the olive, vine, evergreen oak and carob. Use and reduction of the remaining forests has produced many variants of different degradation and regeneration stages, chief amongst which is maquis (low bush). Vegetation removal in different periods has led to soil degradation, erosion and alluviation and badlands are found in Spain, the Italian Apennines and other areas. Extensive terracing on hillsides and check dams across gullies and stream channels were built to check soil from slipping downwards and to replace damaging practices of ploughing down rather than across slopes.

Dispersed farms, where each family lives at a distance from neighbours, are generally associated with poorer, moist hill environments and pastoral economies, and were perhaps the product of piecemeal clearance of waste in small family plots, a pattern retained owing to its convenience for herding. Farm dispersal and bocage (small to medium-sized fields enclosed by hedges) are widely found together in the 'Atlantic ends' of Europe, in Galicia, Brittany, Ireland, north-west Germany and the Norwegian littoral, for example. Although sometimes attributed to 'Celtic' influences, bocage landscapes in these areas seem to be different in age and origin, suggesting that economic adjustment to ecological conditions, rather than ethnic traditions, is the main determinant. In some parts of Atlantic Europe there was a tradition of hamlets (farm clusters without churches or other institutions) and small cultivated infields which seem to have been progressively enclosed and absorbed into the bocage.

The contrast between dispersed and nucleated settlement is not always clear cut. Old hamlets and dispersed farms are often associated and apparently coeval, as in Brittany, and outlying farms frequently occur around old villages as a result of agrarian reforms in recent centuries. Enclosure of open fields and farm dispersal from villages commenced as early as the thirteenth century in England, influenced Denmark in the late eighteenth century and many parts of Europe in the twentieth century. Villages became increasingly anachronistic but have persisted through physical and social inertia. Patterns of settlement evolution are generally convoluted and imperfectly understood. There is some evidence, for example, that the English nucleated village and open-field system may have developed between the tenth and thirteenth centuries through a planned concentration of isolated farmsteads and hamlets scattered over an estate. This pattern is indeed suggested in other countries, and hence, where nucleation and dispersal occur together, the dispersal may sometimes be older than the nuclei.

In southern Europe, areas characterized by either nucleated villages, hamlets, dispersed farms or distinctive combinations of these basic types form

1.4   Eastern Ireland: borders of the counties of Kildare and Wicklow

A bocage type of landscape is characteristic of the level, drift-covered lowlands of east central Ireland. Clustered rural settlements occur (as in foreground) but most farms are dispersed and the large, rectangular fields of permanent grassland are enclosed by banks and hedges, with many scattered trees along the field boundaries sometimes giving a misleading impression of a well-wooded landscape. The Agricultural Improvement of the 18th and 19th centuries had deep impact here, often eradicating the lingering remnants of medieval open-field village organization. However, the origins of farm dispersal and enclosure are not everywhere clearly traceable and some appreciable continuity of ancient, Celtic dispersed settlements patterns may have occurred. Unlike many bocage areas, this fieldscape is relatively stable. Contemporary problems include stream and ground-water pollution, mainly from intensive agricultural activities, and uncontrolled house building along country roads which often amounts to virtual suburbanization. Valued habitats, such as raised bogs, are also being damaged and removed. (Photograph: F. Aalen) a complicated, multi-causal spatial pattern. Marked agglomerations show some correlation with arid southern areas such as New Castile in Spain, southern Italy and Greece, while smaller villages, hamlets and dispersed farms are more characteristic of pluviose Spain, central Italy, the Po plain and the Alps. Most of the Mediterranean lowlands were closely settled and ecologically transformed in ancient times, while the highlands were relatively untouched save by transhumant groups and the demand for timber. However, the collapse of Roman and Byzantine power made the lowlands vulnerable and dangerous, while the mountains offered refuge and security. Defensive and other considerations thus often led to the concentration of the farming population in compact, hilltop villages characteristically associated with open-field cultivation on scattered, irregular plots.

Over the last two centuries or so, economic and ecological processes have combined to seriously undermine Mediterranean rural life, especially in the marginal mountain environments where fluctuations outside a narrow band of population density could lead to a self-reinforcing deterioration in the productive potential of landscapes (McNeill 1992). Emigration and shortages of labour in the villages made it impossible to maintain the land efficiently. Increasingly, terrace and irrigation systems collapsed, fields and buildings were abandoned and transhumance declined, all of which encouraged spontaneous recuperation of natural vegetation successions. Especially since World War II, economic development in the Mediterranean has essentially entailed intensification in the more fertile lowlands and continued abandonment of poorer mountain lands, both tendencies exacerbated by EEC agrarian policies.

Europe's landscapes were not only influenced by sedentary farming activities. Shifting cultivation (swidden or 'slash and burn') based on periodic clearing and burning of forest patches for crops and animal grazing was practised in many areas of Europe from prehistoric to modern times, especially on pioneering frontiers and in agriculturally marginal zones. Slavic tribes had colonized the northern coniferous forest belt in Russia through swiddening, and varieties of swidden cultivation persisted on poor soils in remote hill areas of central Europe and in the forests of Ardennes until recent times. Burning of rough vegetation on moors and bogs was also widespread; indeed, spring burning of heather continues on hill grazing areas in Atlantic Europe, and burning of forest and maquis is still widespread in the Mediterranean. From prehistoric times, swidden cultivation was widely used to produce grain in the coniferous forests of interior Finland and northern Sweden and was accompanied by hunting and fishing; it remained of immense economic and ecological significance until the period of industrialization, when population pressure led to its replacement by field cultivation and manuring of soils. Swidden has deeply modified the European coniferous forest belt, with tracts of deciduous forest (birch, aspen and alder) marking the old clearances (Raumolin 1987).

Within historic land-use systems, vast pasturing systems were required for the rearing of livestock. Summer and winter sheep pastures, for example, were often hundreds of kilometres apart and varieties of livestock, such as pigs and geese, were grazed in distant forests. Transhumant pastoralism played a key role in linking up the lowlands with the mountains. Its organization varied

1.5 North Andros, Greece

Although the island of Andros possesses some of the most fertile and populous areas in the whole of the Cyclades, its northern region is mainly rocky, dusty and bare upland dissected by narrow, steep valleys and in the summer months directly exposed to prolonged north-east gales. Dispersed settlement and pastoral pursuits reflect environmental contraints and the medieval settlement of Albanians in the region. Villages are few and the scattered farmsteads, with their characteristic Aegean flat roofs, are sited mainly on the sheltered slopes and in hollows: many have been abandoned owing to depopulation in modern times. Farmed land is enclosed by low stone walls and patches of poorly developed terracing occur which are difficult to date and now largely neglected and decaying. Grazing of cattle, sheep and goats is the major land use and restrains the spread of maquis, but the landscape is inhospitable and ecologically vulnerable. (Photograph: F. Aalen) with local relief and human/historical conditions but, typically, it involved the summer movement of herders and livestock from permanent lowland settlements to mountain pastures where herders lived temporarily in huts. Inverse transhumance also occurred, with herds moving down in winter from highland villages to lowlands in order to escape the cold. Long-distance, large-scale and highly regulated herd movements existed in, for example, the Iberian peninsula, southern France, peninsula Italy, the Carpathians, and among the Vlachs of the Balkan peninsula. Short-range, local movements around mountain villages to exploit available resources was also a common strategy, found in the Alps, the Carpathians and Norwegian mountains, and could give rise to a whole spectrum of sites and temporary settlement features, graded from regularly used structures in the vicinity of the village to remote and rarely visited highland sites.

European mountain pastoral life is everywhere in decline and mountain areas as a whole are experiencing depopulation. But it is clear from folk-life traditions, archaeology and place names that transhumance was once part and parcel of peasant life throughout the hilly and mountainous parts of the continent, and its environmental legacy is considerable. In phases of population growth, seasonal sites were often the prelude to permanent settlement if the environment could be sufficiently improved, while in other areas, long after transhumance ceased, remote, upland grazing grounds may still be recognizable as verdant patches produced by centuries of dunging. The constant movement of millions of animals must also have played a major part in the dispersal of plants and insects.

The rise of the modern capitalist economy within Europe and its evolution into industrialism had far-reaching effects on human-nature interactions as new landscapes emerged suited to changing levels and patterns of development. Indeed, the first revolutionary effects were felt through agrarian reforms and 'rationalization' of the countryside by enclosure movements, privatization of formerly communal resources, land reclamation and improvement, and growing migration of the rural population to urban centres (Claval 1990). The area of agricultural land significantly increased through both piecemeal reclamation of marginal land such as the Irish bogs and extensive reclamation projects such as on the Lüneburg heath in Germany and the heaths of western Jutland in Denmark. The Romanian steppe was ploughed up for cereal production, there was a marked expansion of farming on the Spanish Meseta and considerable advance of settlement in the forested valleys of northern Sweden and the Finnish forests. Major drainage projects were undertaken such as the Zuider Zee, the Pontine marshes, and the vast Prypec marshes in Poland, traditionally a major barrier to east–west movement (Pounds 1985).

As the economic demands of the main population centres grew in the nineteenth century, there was a tendency for concentric zones of land-use intensity to develop around them; densely populated arable and urban cores emerge with sparsely settled, forested peripheries and mixed conditions in between. These patterns are observable at several different scales, ranging from local centres to industrial regions and, ultimately, a continent-wide adjustment to the urban-industrial core region in north-western Europe.

1.6 Hallingdal, central Norway

Hallingdal is one of the long, narrow dales that penetrate the vast barren plateaux of the Hardangervidda from the east. Forestry here is combined with farming and, because the area lies above the limits of normal crops, farm production is mainly confined to hay and a few potatoes. Farmsteads and improved land (*inmark*) are scattered in forest clearings on the floor and slopes of the dale, particularly the south-facing slope, and are associated with patches of glacial drift. There is no stone walling; stones have been cleared into heaps and field boundaries are inconspicuous. The parallel linear features in the fields are wire hay-drying fences. Outlying fields (*utmark*) extended to the edge of the mountain plateau (c. 1000m), but many have been abandoned. Moorland above the dale was important as summer pasture for cattle. Each valley farm had two or three summer farms (*seters*) which produced butter and cheese and kept cattle away from the *inmark* during the growing season. Grazing, sustained from prehistoric times, modified the ecology of the uplands and retained their open character, with grass-dominated meadows flourishing where utilization was strongest. Hallingskarvet (in background) is a well-defined fjell massif with bare rock surfaces and permanent snow patches. Hallingdal was isolated until 1909 when the Bergen–Oslo railway opened, arresting depopulation and stimulating tourism (especially winter sports around Geilo) and minor industries. Summer farming has declined and *seter* huts are now used as second homes or by tourists. (Photograph: Telemark Flyselskap A/S)

'Progress' was thus widely felt but it did not necessarily homogenize the landscape. Fernand Braudel (1986) emphasizes that the old mosaic of the French countryside, 'that undeniable, even defiant diversity', was essentially preserved and the industrial revolution by encouraging more efficient and specialized agriculture may have further differentiated rural landscapes. F.M.L. Thompson (1985) argues that nineteenth century industrialization, normally regarded as highly destructive of the English landscape, had less impact than generally believed. Manufacturing was increasingly concentrated in towns and working-class housing was very compact, unlike garden city suburbs of the twentieth century. A countryman of 1830 visiting Britain in 1901 would not have noticed any widespread unfamiliar features.

Concern for the preservation of the beauty and diversity of Europe's landscapes developed mainly in the twentieth century; it grew substantially in post-war decades and is now allying itself with the wider search for environmental protection and sustainability. There is general awareness that landscapes are rapidly changing and that their local distinctiveness and long-term productivity are being diminished by diverse economic and social forces, such as more mechanized and intensive farming and forestry and a general standardization of culture, often encouraged by national and European government policies. To retain their diversity and remain productive enough to meet the rapidly growing and conflicting demands of humanity, landscapes must be managed with due care and understood and respected as wholes, a melding of culture and nature, the product of human activities individual and collective, past and present, and of nature's reactions and independent rhythms. This holistic approach does not come readily to us; it is not encouraged by routine experiences and rarely inculcated by traditional education. As Ruskin complains: 'we do not in our everyday life have a bird's eye point of view on the variegated mosaic of the world's surface and a broad grasp of its fulness'.

Chapter 2

Ecological pattern and process at the landscape scale

B.H. Green

Introduction

Ecology as a scientific discipline developed at the same time as nature conservation and provided the theoretical basis for conservation management with its practical manipulation of species populations and plant and animal communities. As in all areas of human endeavour, beliefs (or in science, theories) have always had a far greater influence on actions than the facts. Given sufficiently convincing weight of evidence against them, beliefs, and theories, can however change over time with profound effects on practical action based on them. After a long period largely dominated by ideas now nearly a century old, ecology in the last twenty years has undergone a major transformation in its basic precepts, fed by a surge of new ideas derived more from widespread empirical research rather than deduced from belief and academic theorising. Links have also been forged with cognate disciplines. Landscape ecology is one of the significant products of these changes. It is providing both the intellectual underpinning and the rationale for widening the horizons of nature conservation into the more holistic approaches of landscape management.

Landscape ecology developed in Germany and The Netherlands by a coming together of geographers concerned with the pattern and history of landscape features and ecologists interested in those ecological patterns and processes which take place at a larger scale than the community and ecosystem. Accounts of the development of the subject are given in the pioneering texts of Zonneveld (1995), Naveh and Lieberman (1984) and Forman and Godron (1986). More recent developments are recorded in Forman (1995) and Farina (1998). Despite the important integrating agency of these texts, the newly evolving discipline is still somewhat of a miscellany of different subjects lacking a clear core theoretical structure. But principles with important practical applications are beginning to emerge. Essentially it is concerned with three main areas of study:

- determination of pattern in landscapes and of the resources and forces which determine it, both natural and anthropogenic;

- the response of species, including humans, to this pattern, both in their movement and population dynamics; and
- the nature of energy and nutrient flows between the components of the landscape pattern (Green 1996).

Pattern in landscapes

Resources

There are two main causes of landscape pattern: variation in resources and disturbance. Early ecological research was primarily concerned with the former. Analysis of variation and classification of like types together is an essential prerequisite of understanding in almost any field of human endeavour. Thus early ecologists, particularly plant ecologists, were very much concerned with the identification of plant communities and their relationships to each other. Quite different assemblages of species obviously occur where there are different environmental resources. At the global level the availability of water, determined by climatic factors, is a major determinant of the prevailing vegetation, which, in turn, largely determines the communities of animals which are dependent on vegetation for food and shelter. Where water is readily available forests predominate; where it is not trees are excluded and scrub, grassland or deserts prevail; where water is superabundant, fens, bogs and marshes develop over the waterlogged terrain.

The availability of light, the other main resource of photosynthetic production, is another determinant of vegetation: but, since it is more universally available except where limited by the shade of trees, it is not such an important factor at the larger scales of variation. Nor is carbon dioxide, for the same reason. It is the availability of the nutrient elements required to elaborate proteins and all the other chemicals of living organisms from the basic carbohydrates produced by photosynthesis that are key determinants of both production and the distribution of different types of plant species, and of the plant communities they came to constitute. The availability of these nutrient elements depends very much on the underlying geology and the soils it produces. The most important variations are those in the major nutrient elements nitrogen, phosphorus and potassium, and less directly, of calcium, which determines the pH of the soil and the extent to which the plants can take up the major nutrient elements. Factors which constrain production, for example, salinity, can also affect vegetation. Within, therefore, any extensive tract of forest, grassland or wetland, there are likely to be soil, or edaphic, variations, which are often reflected in the presence of different species with adaptations to them constituting a resource mosaic of different plant communities.

There was once a tendency to believe that the same species and the same communities always occurred in a predictable, determined way where there were similar environmental conditions. Clearly, this only applies within geographically defined floristic and faunistic regions, for evolution has operated independently within continents separated by ocean or mountain barriers. Species from quite unrelated taxonomic groups have often evolved into the same niches, providing remarkable examples of convergent evolution. The Atlantic and Pacific mangroves, or the Old and New World vultures, for example, come from genetically very different stock but are remarkably similar in structure. Many species introduced by man to new regions beyond their natural distribution often thrive there better than native species in similar niches. In particular, species evolved in the old hard schools of continental evolution are usually better competitors than those of islands or other isolated land masses.

Even within a floristic or faunistic region, however, we now know that species can and do assemble together in many different combinations. The same piece of ground made available for colonization at different times may produce very different plant communities depending on the weather of a particular year, the coincidence of a good seed year for particular species, whether pigs rooted there, or even whether a flock of birds happened to settle on and fertilize a site with their droppings. Chance or stochastic events of this kind are now seen to be of great importance in determining the nature of ecosystem pattern and processes. In particular, disturbance, far from being seen as an unusual event usually attributed to human intervention, is now appreciated as a quite normal and natural process which is vital in determining landscape pattern and species diversity.

Disturbance

Superimposed on the pattern of plant and animal communities determined by resources there is thus another, more unpredictable, dynamic pattern generated by natural disturbances such as fire, flood, windstorms, avalanches, landslides and volcanic activity. Species have evolved in relation to disturbance regimes, which vary in their frequency, intensity, predictability, seasonality and size, as well as in relation to the availability of resources (Fig. 2.1) (Grime 1979, Huston 1994). Within any landscape we can identify a mosaic of overlapping resource and disturbance patches, all characterized by their distinctive assemblages of similarly evolved species (Fig. 2.2) (Green 1996). Whilst disturbance is largely a chance event, landscape characteristics can influence the nature of disturbances in a predictable, determined way similar to the way in which resource patches are mostly determined by geology and topography. In mountains, for example, avalanche tracks along gullies are often clearly visible as vertical stripes of grassland in the dominant forest; dry, south-facing slopes are more vulnerable to lightning fires and likely to be vegetated with pines or other fire-evolved species; bluffs and escarpments exposed to the prevailing wind are more likely to lose trees in storms and support open grassland, scrub and other successional vegetation. In valleys, floods and the deposition of sandbanks and dunes similarly bring about their own characteristic disturbance regimes and communities. Elsewhere on wide river valleys, or on plateaux and peneplains, natural disturbance events may be less frequent. Human disturbance in such areas can, however, be very considerable.

In modern agricultural landscapes both the intensity and extent of human disturbance are generally far greater than any natural disturbance regimes. Such landscapes are typically a mix of annually disturbed cropland, less

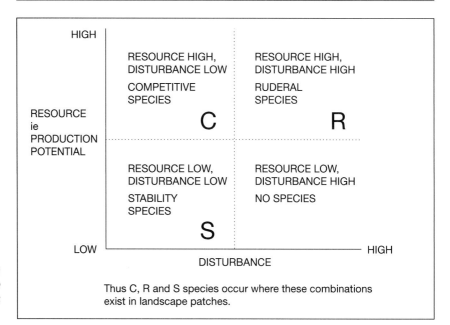

2.1 Interaction between resource and disturbance patches in landscapes

Thus C, R and S species occur where these combinations exist in landscape patches.

2.2 Species life history strategies and landscape disturbance patterns

intensively disturbed grassland, often spontaneously generated from wild communities, and remnant patches of relatively undisturbed original vegetation. The disturbed areas represent the matrix in which relatively undisturbed remnant fragments of more natural vegetation cover remain. In landscapes subject to more natural disturbance regimes the opposite is usually the case; relatively undisturbed areas form the matrix in which disturbance patches are set. In forested landscapes modern clear-cutting silvicultural systems usually lie somewhere between these extremes. In all landscapes disturbance produces a shifting mosaic of ecosystem patches, with many being in a non-equilibrium successional state of recovery and usually relatively few in an equilibrium climax state (Sousa 1984, Pickett & White 1985).

The response of species to landscape pattern

The richness in species of agricultural landscapes depends very much on the nature and scale of the human disturbance regimes. If they are not too intensive or extensive, then viable wildlife populations may survive in both the farmed land and in any reasonably large remnant patches of the original vegetation set amongst it. Surveys generally show that the larger these isolated patches are, the more species they contain (e.g., Moore & Hooper 1975). This may be because the larger patches contain more habitats, or simply that they sample a greater number of species. It has also been proposed (MacArthur & Wilson 1967) that it is a consequence of species population size determined by rates of immigration and extinction. This Island Biogeographic Theory predicts that the larger of such habitat islands are more likely to contain more species, for they permit larger populations more likely to be augmented by colonizations and less likely to become depleted by extinctions through random population fluctuations.

Empirical evidence confirms this prediction and suggests that in smaller patches populations of some species do indeed seem regularly to be threatened or even to become extinct. If the intervening farmland between the smaller and larger patches permits the surplus individuals from the larger patches with more viable populations to colonize the smaller patches, their smaller populations may be thus sustained, or replaced again after local extinction. It has been demonstrated that a number of species populations of patchy landscapes, notably farm landscapes, consist in this way of a number of small sub-populations, which are dependent on the larger, aggregate, or meta-population (Opdam 1991). The size and isolation of patches thus determines the likelihood of their recolonization.

Whether patches serve as sources of surplus, colonizing individuals, or sinks where they are eventually lost, depends on a number of attributes. Not only patch size, location and the nature of the intervening matrix are important but probably also their linking with one another by habitat corridors (Fig. 2.3). Intuitively we would expect such linkages as hedges, ditches, field banks, headlands, tracks and verges to act not only as corridors or stepping stones between patches, but as habitats in themselves. Such corridors do indeed seem to provide habitat and to facilitate passage for some species, but not others (Saunders & Hobbs 1991, Bennett 1999). Some suggest, however, that they may not be beneficial; serving to facilitate the spread of pests, expose species to predation and even act as sinks which drain the overall meta-population of the region.

Our own species is equally responsive to landscape pattern. Both landscape evaluation exercises and the design of gardens and parks suggest we favour open savannah-like landscapes with groups of trees and grassland. It has been proposed that this is atavistic, reflecting our origins in savannahs and need for knowledge of prospect, refuge and hazard for our survival (Appleton 1975). English parishes were frequently pragmatically circumscribed in relation

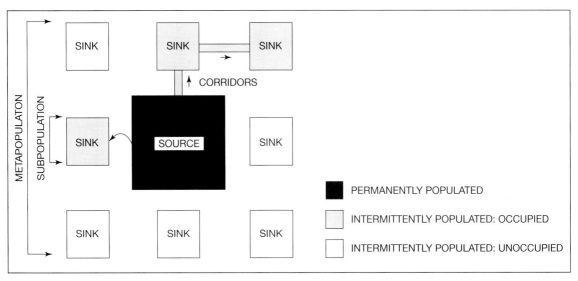

2.3 Metapopulations in fragmented landscapes

to the topography so that each village had its portion of better land for crops, hill grazing and riverside meadows. Forests and common grazing lands were usually the residue left on the more infertile soils. Traditional farming thus incidentally provided the savannah/parkland landscapes we cherish. Modern farming, however, is no longer constrained by the old limiting factors of poor drainage, low fertility and difficult terrain; as a result the landscape heterogeneity generated by the traditional systems is now either being steam-rollered into homogenous prairies of crop monocultures or abandoned back to scrub and forest.

Nutrient and energy flows in landscapes

The sustainability of the first farming in the river valleys of the Middle East was dependent on the transport and discharge of the nutrients in the alluvial silt of annual floods to replace those harvested in the crops. Moving away from such restricted landscape locations was made possible by utilizing the landscape nutrient flows in the dung of animals. By virtue of their mobility animals are an important agency by which nutrients and energy are moved between landscape components. In African savannahs, for example, antelope, buffalo and other hoofed animals commonly rest and sleep in the shade of the clumps of trees where they also dung and urinate. Large amounts of nutrients are thus concentrated on to these landscape resource patches, which in consequence are able to sustain more productive vegetation. The same phenomenon has been documented on the New Forest of the UK (Putman *et al.* 1991). Before crop rotations, before the widespread use of legumes, before the importation of guano from Peru and long before synthetic nitrogen fertilizer, outfield-infield systems of farming were essential in Europe for hundreds of years in order to maintain the fertility of the croplands. Stock were grazed on poor heaths and downlands during the day and then folded to dung on the fallow crop fields at night.

The enrichment of the crop fields was at the expense of the heaths and downs, which were impoverished and, sometimes, desertified by this nutrient pumping. Their species diversity, now so cherished, was however a direct result of it. Their infertility constrains the growth of competitive, dominant plants and allows a wide variety of less competitive species to coexist. Many small isolated nature reserves now attempt to maintain examples of the old heaths and downlands, but enclosed grazing does not remove the nutrients. Effective conservation here is dependent on maintaining all the components of the old landscape system. It was sustainable only at the landscape scale.

Fire is also a major agency of nutrient and energy transfer in landscapes and its operation is also greatly affected by the integrity of landscape components. Isolated oak savannahs in the North American Midwest, for example, are now burnt much less frequently than when they were extensive and continuous. Then the probabilities of natural lightning igniting a fire and of the fire spreading were both high. Fires sometimes ran for hundreds of miles. Fragmentation resulting from agricultural reclamation has dramatically altered the fire regime by reducing the likelihood of small patches being struck and by intervening firebreaks of farmland between them. As a result they are passing through a natural succession to dense forest (Sharpe 1987). Big ecological changes are thus taking place without any changes in ambient environmental conditions other than patch size (Fig. 2.4).

Other changes in landscape components can have equally profound effects on nutrient flows. Erosion and natural drainage move nutrients, both solid and in solution, from one part of the landscape to another under the power of gravity. Riverine forests and reedbeds naturally act as buffers to such nutrient flows into rivers, removing quantities of nitrogen and other nutrients through both denitrification and its incorporation into the biomass. Removing such buffer strips by extending farmland to the very edge of the river bank can result in considerable nutrient losses into the river and its consequent

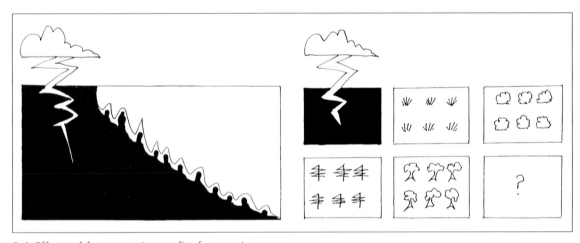

2.4 Effects of fragmentation on fire frequencies

eutrophication. Leaving relatively narrow buffer strips of grass can greatly reduce these flows (Moorby & Cook 1992). Other linear features, such as hedges, can also affect nutrient particulate and water flows, often improving water quality and helping to control erosion. They can, of course, also be effective windbreaks.

The practical application of ecological theory

When ecology began to develop as a scientific discipline at the turn of the twentieth century it was strongly influenced by long-standing beliefs in the balance of nature – the idea that all living organisms are mutually independent and come together into complexly interacting communities in equilibrium with prevailing environmental conditions. Early influential ecologists, such as Clements, saw the climatic climax community as the ultimate equilibrium expression of the regional potential of vegetation and interpreted more dynamic communities as transient – as orderly determined primary or secondary succession to the stable climax. In this framework disturbances were seen essentially as means by which the development of the climatic climax community was frustrated for varying periods of time. Other ecologists of the time, such as Tansley and Gleason, were uneasy with these ideas but they none the less remained influential for a very long time. In National Parks, nature reserves and other protected areas, disturbances were seen as a threat to the equilibrium communities and something to be prevented. Non-interference, laissez-faire policies of leaving Nature to itself dominated conservation thinking. Fire control was, for example, a major policy objective in National Parks in the United States. In European and North American National Parks there has likewise been a great reluctance to control deer and other herbivores, despite their manifest over-grazing of grasslands, scrub and forest in the absence of predators such as wolves, themselves controlled as undesirable 'bad' species, in disregard of the general principle of non-interference.

The consequences of those policies have often been disastrous. With all fires suppressed, the deep litter of dead vegetation which accumulates in grasslands and forests comes to constitute such a fuel load that, sooner or later, ignition and fires become impossible to control and burn far more fiercely and damagingly than when naturally occurring on shorter cycles. Because of this the National Park Service in the United States was forced to change its fire control policy to a fire management policy of which prescribed burns are now an important part. The consequences of this new approach have not always been easy. Fires left to burn in Yellowstone National Park in 1988 raged over millions of hectares, but recovery has been rapid and unexpected changes in species populations and communities have ensued (Budiansky 1995).

With ecosystems now interpreted as generally being in various successional stages of recovery from disturbance, rather than in an equilibrium state, objections to management intervention are clearly more difficult to justify. Further, the human interventions responsible for creating and maintaining cultural landscapes can be seen to be just forms of disturbance analogous to those occurring more naturally. Human disturbances frequently differ substantially in kind from those naturally occurring in their dimensions of extent, frequency and intensity and therefore in their environmental impact, but they are not fundamentally different in their nature. In this context conservation management can be seen to be focused not on eliminating disturbance and ignoring the cultural in favour of the natural, but as the manipulation of disturbance and amelioration of its effects in creating habitat fragmentation and discontinuity.

The relatively small size and continuing isolation of protected areas can significantly change their disturbance regimes and makes them ever more vulnerable to island biogeographic effects and edge effects such as pollution, and drainage; and also, ever more difficult to manage. It is being increasingly realized that they can only be maintained by planning and management at the landscape scale. It is only at this scale that sustainability is a meaningful concept. Ways have to be found to link production and protection areas in landscapes not only physically with hedgerows, waterways and other corridors, but economically as well. The old European outfield–infield system of farming did this and there are indications that new types of farm enterprise diversification into equestrian activities, golf courses, sailing and other recreational pursuits can have similar physical and economic benefits. This integration of land uses will require planning and management at a variety of scales, with plans and policies nesting together hierachically from field, farm and district to regional level. To achieve this, to devise, create and maintain new landscapes, natural and social scientists will have to abandon the insularity of their subjects and interact and collaborate in a much more interdisciplinary way. Landscape ecologists, with their holistic and inter-disciplinary approach, are well placed to meet and lead this challenge.

Chapter 3

An environmental classification of European landscapes

R. G. H. Bunce

Introduction

Classification is an essential prerequisite for effective landscape evaluation, planning and management. In examining the representation of individual threatened landscapes in a protected areas network, for example, it is necessary to ensure that similar landscapes are compared with each other, otherwise the range of variability is so great that comparisons are invalid, as described by Watkins & Bunce (1996). Thus it is not possible to compare a Mediterranean landscape in Crete with a boreal landscape in northern Norway as they are inherently different. Such comparisons commonly have policy implications. Some of the landscape classes that are identified may have no representation of designated sites, either because of national policies, or because they have been overlooked. In Britain, a good example of this problem was provided by the setting up of National Scenic Areas in Scotland. The selection was made by a process of expert judgement. However, it completely omitted the Flow Country of the extreme north. These flat boglands, though visually uninspiring to many people, were subsequently identified as being unique in landscape terms as well as for their biodiversity. They were ignored because of their lack of striking mountain features.

In addition to the description of landscapes, a classification framework is required for two other principal purposes. First, threatened landscapes need objective data to be recorded in order to assess whether the type of changes taking place are affecting the quality of the component elements which characterize them. Such procedures must be statistical, so that real changes can be distinguished from either opinion or background noise. Environmental classification using multivariate methodologies enables representative samples to be selected from defined landscapes in order to assess change. This can be done at a broad level by using data from historical aerial photographs or by using historical data from previous ground surveys.

Second, because the pressure on rural environments operates across national frontiers, it is necessary to have a standardized modelling procedure for assessing the potential impact of policy scenarios on rural landscapes. The effect of those scenarios can then be assessed in order to identify appropriate policies to maintain the characteristics of the landscapes.

Approaches to landscape classification

A distinction has long been made between broad kinds of different landscapes. Cobbett (1830) recognized 'bosky' (wooded) and 'champion' (open) farmland – a classification which is still in common use in France as *bocage* and *campagne*. These were still recognized as two of thirteen main landscape types in an early modern assessment of European landscapes (Meeus *et al*. 1990). An elaboration of this classification scheme into thirty landscape classes was made in the first European state of the environment report (Stanners & Bourdeau 1995) (Table3.1). There have been many assessments of landscapes like these across Europe but nearly all of them have been essentially subjective, involving expert judgement. They are not therefore reproducible and consistent, being dependent upon the experience of the authors. The approach described below has as its main objective to provide a statistical framework that overrides opinions and therefore enables objective comparisons to be made. The resulting categories therefore may not fit

Table 3.1 A descriptive assessment of European landscapes

Tundras
1. Arctic tundra
2. Forest Tundra

Taigas or Forest Landscapes
3. Boreal Swamp
4. Northern Taiga
5. Central Taiga
6. Southern Taiga
7. Subtaiga

Highlands and Mountains
8. Nordic Highlands
9. Mountains

Enclosed Landscapes with Hedges/Bocage
10. Atlantic Bocage
11. Atlantic Semi-Bocage
12. Mediterranean Semi-Bocage

Open Fields
13. Atlantic Openfields
14. Continental Openfields

15. Aquitaine Openfields
16. Former Openfields
17. Collective Openfields
18. Mediterranean Openlands

Regional Landscapes
19. Coltura Promiscua
20. Montados or Dehesa
21. Delta
22. Huerta
23. Polder
24. Kampen
25. Poland's Strip Fields

Steppes
26. Puszta
27. Steppe

Arid Landscapes
28. Semi-desert
29. Sand-desert

Terrace Landscapes
30. Terraces

Source: Meeus *et al*. 1990

boundaries derived by expert judgement, for example, between the Atlantic and Continental climates described by Kendrew (1953). They do, however, much more effectively fulfil a variety of practical purposes in landscape planning and management.

A multivariate methodology

A fundamental problem in the assessment of landscape character is that the underlying environmental parameters vary continuously and they are the product of many interacting factors. The aesthetic appreciation of scenery, which involves perception, is nevertheless often based upon objective measurable factors, such as the length of tree lines or walls. The task of landscape description is to divide the continuous variation into classes that are convenient to handle. Such divisions are arbitrary since there is no evidence of discontinuity, except in some exceptional cases. The majority of studies have used overt expert judgement to describe, in order to define and evaluate landscapes, as described by Watkins & Bunce (1996), although quantitative methods are now available. Multivariate methodology is capable of providing a framework for objective assessment, which is essential if cultural differences are to be transcended and appropriate policies developed. It is also possible subjectively to define units within the objective framework, as has been already carried out by overlaying the European classes with the potential natural vegetation map of the continent.

The Great Britain land classification

In Britain the Institute of Terrestrial Ecology, now the Centre for Ecology and Hydrology, has developed a Land Classification System over the last 25 years based on the construction of environmental strata from widely available cartographic data. The system was developed initially in local studies in northern England (Bunce, Morrell & Stel 1975) and was later tested in a regional study in Cumbria (Bunce & Smith 1978). The principle behind the classification is that the major significant ecological and landscape variables are associated with and dependent upon environmental variables. The statistical procedure used formalizes these relationships and was used to classify the whole of Great Britain (Fig. 3.1).

The presence of environmental variables, such as geology, land use, altitude classes, tree cover and water features, was recorded in grid squares from published maps in much the same way as plants in a quadrat. In 1977, 1212 1-km squares on a 15 x 15 km grid were used for the base classification which was subsequently extended to all squares in Great Britain (Bunce *et al.* 1996a). The grid squares were then successively divided into 2^n groups on the basis of the similarity of their environmental data characteristics using a multivariate ordination technique originally developed for vegetation. This methodology – TWINSPAN (Two Way Indicator Species Analysis) (Hill 1979) – created relatively homogeneous, recognizable assemblies of 1-km squares at the division level of 32 groups, termed 'Land Classes'. These have subsequently been used as a framework for national field surveys of landscape, land use and vegetation data in 1978, 1984, 1990 and 1998.

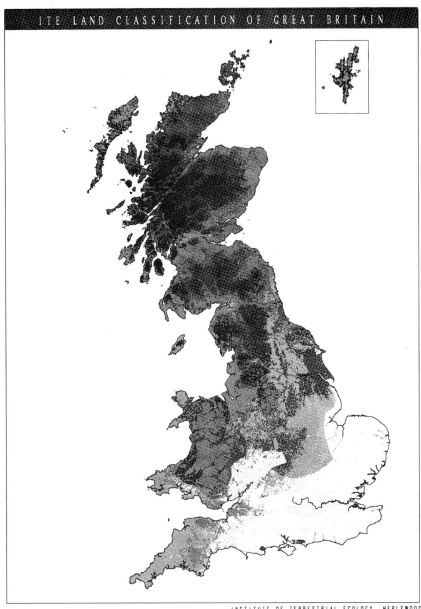

ITE LAND CLASSIFICATION OF GREAT BRITAIN

3.1 The Great Britain Land Classification

INSTITUTE OF TERRESTRIAL ECOLOGY, MERLEWOOD

The results described in Barr *et al.* (1993) show how the procedure has been used to assess stock and change of landscape features, land use, land cover and vegetation. It has also been used as a basis for landscape description in Great Britain, as shown by Benefield & Bunce (1982), and for monitoring landscape features, for example in Barr & Whittaker (1987). Although there are many sources of information on specific land-cover features from responsible agencies, such as forestry from the Forestry Commission, this project is the first to produce integrated, statistically derived figures for the entire British countryside. While not optimal for any given group, it enables disparate data to be linked through the common environment classification. Thus data for birds, moths and freshwater invertebrates can be placed on a common format and compared with the landscape divisions set up by other agencies. A delivery system, the Countryside Information System, has been developed (Haines-Young *et al.* 1994) to provide ready access to the results of the successive surveys, as well as the other appropriate information. Subsequent descriptions of the landscape character of England and Wales have used variations of the methodology (Countryside Commission 1996).

The European classification

At a European level, it is necessary to develop a balance in the environmental factors which feed into the classification system. Even within regional classifications, such as that carried out in Britain, the dominant elements which determine the broad structure of the classification are climate and altitude, although many other factors such as geology were included. At the European scale, however, data sets describing even simple parameters such as geology are not consistent across frontiers and are also very variable in quality. It was therefore decided that to achieve most of the objectives required at the European scale, climatic and altitudinal data should form the basis of the classification, together with certain locational information, principally latitude. Subsequent analyses have actually linked the classes determined from these parameters into higher-level groups using potential natural vegetation or land cover from satellite imagery.

The major divisions of the classification (Fig. 3.2) correspond to recognizable divisions of European climate such as Mediterranean or Continental, as described by Kendrew (1953). The statistical procedures were investigated by Jones and Bunce (1985) and were applied to a data set derived from the Climate Research Unit at the University of East Anglia (Hulme *et al.* 1995) which covers a 'Greater European Window' extending east to the Urals and south to Africa. The extensive database contained the 1961 to 1990 mean monthly climate figures for seven climatic variables, for example, rain days in December, and a subset of the data was constructed, chosen by applying Principal Components Analysis, to identify the most important variables. Otherwise the classification is dominated by repeated measures which contain the same information. In addition, three measures of altitude, oceanicity and northing were included. TWINSPAN was used to produce 64 classes using a comparable procedure to that developed by Bunce *et al.* (1996a) for Great Britain. As part of this procedure, the same classification can be applied to 1-km squares that have not initially been classified and an algorithm is also available to carry this out. An appropriate database has been identified to enable this transformation to be undertaken.

European land classes

The classes have been described in terms of their geographical distribution, potential vegetation and land forms (Bunce *et al.* 1996b) and identify some familiar features such as the Cantabrian mountains (Class 40). Other classes are more unexpected, such as the Lusitanian class, which is present in Brittany, south-west England and the extreme west of Holland and Denmark, with an outlier in Galicia in north-west Spain, linked by the dominance of the oceanic influence. The classes have been shown to be highly correlated with individual species distribution patterns, for example of *Vaccinium vitis-idaea* and the arctic-alpine species, *Carex bigelowii*. These descriptions can be progressively increased in their degree of detail, as has been carried out for the Great Britain Land Classes where progressive databases have been built up incorporating features such as vegetation, tree cover and landscape character. The underlying land forms common to the classes can also be used to build up scenarios of change and the influence of local management.

It is useful to analyse the European environment at different levels in the nesting hierarchy of environmental features. Whilst these levels are arbitrary, five different tiers are useful to consider in the present context.

Level 1: biogeographic zones

These could either be existing zones, for example that used by the European Environment Agency, or zones that have been constructed by linking the 64 classes by statistical analysis of common ecological parameters, such as potential vegetation or land cover. The former zonation has been carried out in the DMEER (Digital Map of European Ecological Regions) produced for the European Topic Centre for Nature Conservation and the latter for the MIRABEL (Models for Integrated Review and Assessment of Biodiversity in European Landscapes) project.

Level 2: the 64 European land classes

These classes are appropriate for drawing representative samples as has been proposed in the EUROLUS project (a quantitative assessment of land use, biodiversity and indicators for the wider European countryside), which is currently incorporated in a proposal to the Fifth Framework Programme of the European Union. This project involves the selection of random 1-km squares from the environmental classes present in the fifteen participating countries. Field survey could then be carried out in these sites and figures produced for broad habitats, vegetation and landscape structure for the whole of Europe.

Level 3: landscape

Within both Levels 1 and 2 different landscapes may be present which can be determined, either by statistical analysis or by the more usual application of experience, to identify and interpret relatively homogeneous units. For example, Environmental Class 23, which is unique to Britain and extends from south-west England and Wales, through the Pennines and into the Scottish mountains, will contain contrasting landscapes, due to the interaction of

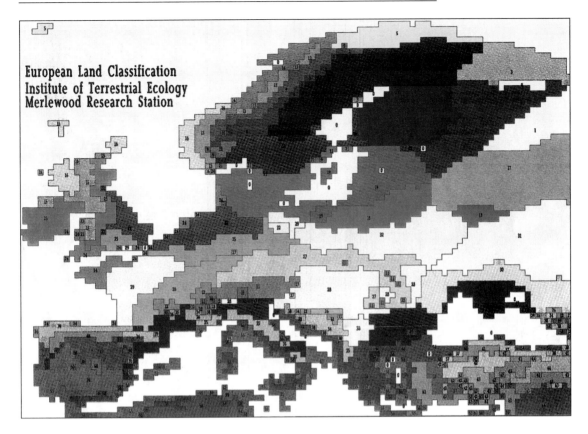

European Land Classification
Institute of Terrestrial Ecology
Merlewood Research Station

3.2 The European Land Classification

local factors, but still remains a valid environmental zone within Europe. Government bodies such as Scottish Heritage and the Countryside Agency have, using intuitive procedures, drawn up such maps which can be related to the European Classification using GIS.

Level 4: biotopes (habitats)

A given landscape will be made up of different combinations of habitats (or vegetation types or biotopes).

Level 5: species

These combine to form habitats, but are not mutually exclusive because a given species may occur in several habitats, in the same way as a habitat may be present in different landscapes.

It is useful to take two examples of the individual classes to give an idea of the way in which the classification could be used as a framework for comparison of landscapes (Fig. 3.3).

3.3 European Land Classes 25 and 40

Example 1: Northern plains and undulating low hills

Class 25 is distributed in central and southern England, northern France, southern Belgium and central Germany and extends into the west of the Czech Republic and Poland. In general the landforms present are lowland river valleys, plains and undulating low hills, and, because it crosses such a wide range of cultural conditions, there are many different recognizable landscapes. The class is nevertheless relatively homogeneous in altitude and climatic factors at a European level. In terms of potential vegetation the class is dominated by beech and oak forest, although the majority of the land surface is now intensively farmed. In Britain the recognizable landscapes would include the New Forest, North Downs, Somerset Levels, Thames Valley and the southern Midlands. In France the landscapes would be mainly the chalk downlands and clay valleys of the Pas de Calais; in Belgium the southern agricultural landscapes as well as the Ardennes. Further east, similar complexes could be identified using regional expertise.

Example 2: Cantabrian mountains

Class 40 is distributed mainly in north-west Spain, but extends into northern Portugal and, in terms of land form, is a complex of mountains and valleys. However, there are strong contrasts in geology, which give rise to different landscapes, further differentiated by regional climatic variation. The potential natural vegetation is highly varied and dependent upon the geology and local climate, with forests of evergreen oak at lower altitudes and Pyrennean oak and beech at higher elevations. There is also heathland and sub-alpine vegetation at high altitudes. The hills of the eastern Cantabrian mountains are usually below 1200 metres and are a mixture of sandstones and limestones with much local variation. In the centre of the chain, the Picos de Europa mountains reach 2500 metres and are a well-known distinctive landscape, but even here there are strong constrasts between the valleys, the mid-slopes and the bare rocky limestone summits. Further to the west, the hills are usually below 1700 metres and are more rounded, being of sandstone and granite.

These two classes demonstrate the necessity of a common framework because in the first case the differences in landscape are primarily due to cultural factors, whereas in the second the variations are caused by underlying environmental parameters. The two examples also indicate how the classification can be used to identify the various characteristic landscapes within the classes. These landscapes can then be validly compared with each other and, using methodologies such as those described in Chapter 10, evaluation can take place. There are inevitably major problems of scale and definition, but at least these units provide an independent basis that is not reliant on personal opinion. The two examples also show that some of the classes are likely to be more variable than others, as has been shown in Great Britain, where East Anglia consists of classes that comprise very little variation in landscape, and north-west Scotland has classes with mountains, crofting land and a highly variable coastline. Nevertheless, these classes are still relatively homogeneous in their environment within Britain. The use of environmental variables to create such zones is described by Bunce *et al.* (1996a) and has the major advantage that it is relatively unchanging, whereas if landscape features are included, then the class of an individual cell can change over time, which confuses the ability to compare and monitor the changes which are taking place.

Scale

These examples of continental and national multivariate landscape classifications illustrate that classifications can be made at a variety of scales, as appropriate for particular objectives. For local planning purposes sampling can be undertaken in smaller grid squares to identify landscapes, or landscape units or elements, right down to the level of the parish (Blankson & Green 1991). Theoretically at least these lower levels could then nest hierarchically with larger landscape units to form a classification analogous, though more artificial, to that for species, genera, families, etc. of living organisms.

Scale is also important in that landscapes described at different scales can reveal very different landscape patterns, which, in turn, can provide an insight into the processes producing the patterns and moulding the landscape (Wiens *et al.* 1986). Here, again, there is an analogy with the analysis of quadrat data in plant ecology where systematic sampling of vegetation at different sample frame sizes can dramatically reveal patterns of plant distribution invisible to the eye and point to the underlying causes such as stolon length or seed scatter (Greig-Smith 1964).

Conclusions

Scepticism about the existence of meaningful landscape units, let alone their classification, has long delayed the development of landscape studies and landscape planning and management. The emergence of The European

Landscape Classification shows that landscapes can be classified and that such classifications can be used, not only to provide a statistically rigorous framework for the evaluation of landscapes, but also to monitor change and co-ordinate other information which may be collected using objective procedures, or be purely descriptive. This is, however, only the beginning of the exploitation of landscape classification for landscape planning and management. As indicated above, there is enormous potential for the development of standardized classification hierarchies and for research into landscape pattern and process to provide even more valuable tools for the planner and manager. The increasing availability of higher-resolution remote sensing data and the cross-linking of landscape data with other spatial databases, such as those produced by the CORINE Programme, will greatly facilitate these activities.

Part Two

Landscapes worthy of protection

Polders

Polder landscapes occur in most reclaimed estuaries and low-lying coastal and inland areas of the world. In Europe, the most characteristic and widespread polder landscapes occur in The Netherlands, a nation that was largely carved from the estuaries of three great European Rivers, the Rhine, Meuse and Schelde, from medieval times on. Their origin and management give them a number of specific attributes: dense waterway and field patterns, dyke systems, windmills, pumping stations, open wetland sceneries and, under low-intensity farming, a variety of saline, brackish and freshwater habitats rich in aquatic and wetland species and especially important to breeding and migrating wildfowl. Their alluvial substrates make them, however, potentially very productive, and consequently large areas have been converted to more intensive crop and livestock farming. The resulting lowered water tables, enrichment and losses of habitats have caused a decline of characteristic biodiversities and wetland sceneries. This tension between the developmental possibilities of agriculture and values pertaining to nature and landscape is typical of the peatland polder areas. Their location close to urban centres also introduces all kinds of (sub)urban stresses. Reconciling agricultural and environmental objectives is difficult, but progress has been made in The Netherlands, both technically and in planning procedures based on the broad commitment of different groups of regional actors.

Chapter 4
Krimpenerwaard, The Netherlands

H.C. Greven and W. Vos

Introduction

The Krimpenerwaard is a peatbog polder located in the western part of The Netherlands, in the province of South-Holland, in the 'Green Heart of Holland' (Fig.4.1). It is a fairly homogeneous open area of mainly agricultural land (grassland) and some small nature reserves, surrounded on three sides by different branches of the river Rhine (the River Lek in the south, the Hollandse IJssel in the northwest, and the peat-brook the Vlist in the east). To the west is the conurbation of the city of Rotterdam. The polder is located between c.1.0 and 2.5 m below sea level, and is drained by seven pumping stations. It comprises approximately 13,000 ha, of which some 15 to 20 per cent is open water. The peat in places reaches depths of more than 10 m. Clayey and clayey-peat soils occur along the rivers. Here, most of the houses and farm

4.1 The Krimpenerwaard situated in the Green Heart of Holland

buildings are concentrated in lines along the foot of the banks of the dikes. In the central part, narrow ribbons of farms and a few elongated villages are laid out on sandy ridges of Pleistocene dunes. In the south, the area receives seepage water from the River Lek, but in the centre and north the polder looses water towards the deeper north-western polders.

The scenery is characterized by openness due to a lack of relief, absence of woods, and the almost parallel bands of buildings, land parcels, embankments and waterways. Open water is everywhere and where no water is visible it is very close beneath the surface. At present less than 1 per cent of the total area is protected as a nature reserve. There are some 350 farm holdings, mainly engaged in dairy farming. The holdings have, on average, about 24 ha and less than 50 cows, which is much less than the normal trend in The Netherlands. Although the land use is intensive, most of the farmers do not produce enough fodder for their dairy stock. Agricultural modernization in the Krimpenerwaard has not kept pace with developments in the rest of the country and until recently only one-quarter of the farms had modern box stalls (Eggink 1994). Industrial activities only occur on the riverbanks, where some ship-building and metal industry firms are established. The Krimpenerwaard landscape altogether constitutes a 'normal' but characteristic Dutch polder landscape with environmental problems, a problematic agricultural future and an increasing urban stress. Practically the whole area contains the nature and landscape qualities of the so-called main ecological network of the Nature Policy Plan of the Netherlands (1990).

The historical geography of the area

Before the closing of the dike system around 1300 AD, the Krimpenerwaard (Fig. 4.2) was regularly flooded during times of high river discharges. The oldest visible landforms on the surface date from the end of the ultimate glacial period more than 10,000 years ago. These so-called *donken* are flattened old river dunes of sand that originate from the then dry river beds. Their summits rise just a little above the surrounding Holocene peat and clay sediments. The dikes, constructed from the early medieval period on, ended the natural sedimentation. Thereafter only occasional sedimentation took place in the polder after dike-bursts. Along the borders of the polder, the results of the latter are still visible in the form of *wielen*, small ponds surrounded by low levees of loamy deposits, frequently under some woodland. Man has reclaimed many of these ponds, sometimes by filling them with rubbish.

As a result of compaction and oxidation of the peat after drainage, the soil surface of the polders has gradually lowered several metres, a process that still continues. It explains why clay and loam deposits as well as sandy *donken* nowadays rise some ten centimetres above the peat. Although the peat may reach a considerable depth, no large peat-excavations have been done.

The first habitation in the former peat bog area was concentrated on the drier parts: the *donken* and the river dunes. From medieval times on, the firmer clay and peat soils along the River Lek and the Hollandse IJssel were also inhabited. From about 1000 AD a systematic reclamation of the marshy

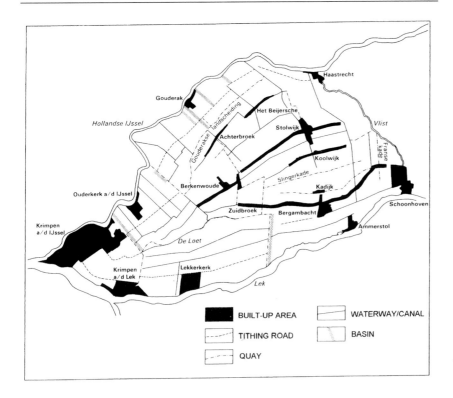

4.2 Topography of the Krimpenerwaard

woodland started along the rivers. Long straight ditches, beginning from the occupied fringes, perpendicular to the reclamation base and parallel to each other on both sides of the parcels of land (with a width of 120 m) drained the area. At the end of each plot, a backside watercourse parallel to the reclamation base was dug to a length of 650 m or a multiple of it. In this way a so-called *slagen* landscape with narrow, but very long parcels was developed (Fig. 4.3). Characteristic features of *slagen* landscapes are tithing roads, back and foreside watercourses, double ribbon-occupation axes, land segregations, blind alleys and numerous parallel ditches (see De Jongh *et al.* 1987). Between the remaining marsh woodland in the centre of the polder and the already reclaimed area a low dike was constructed with a watercourse. This was the so-called 'tithing road' and most of these are still present in their original form, some of them still being unmetalled. The tithe was brought to the landlords by boat and taken by them via the roads. Crossing the land was by bridge. A tree or some shrubs were planted to consolidate the slope. These so-called *hovelingen* indicate the original function of the fairways. In the evolution from 'fairway polder' to 'traffic by road polder' many bridges were replaced by dams.

At the start of the reclamation, ditches drained directly into the rivers, but with increasing subsidence the water had to be lifted from canals and basins up to the river level. This was first done with windmills, but from the mid-nineteenth century with steam engines, and in the twentieth century with diesel engines. Originally, there were no buildings in the polder. Later more land was reclaimed in a similar way and farms were built in ribbons along the

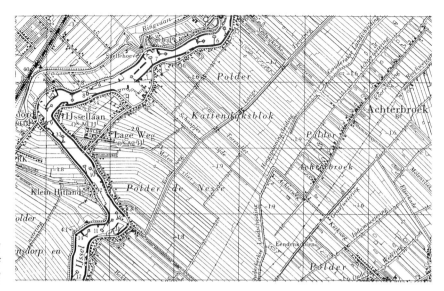

4.3 The so-called 'slagen' landscape of the Krimpenerwaard

river. The reclaimed areas were protected against the water from the not yet reclaimed area in the centre of the polder by a quay. In subsequent centuries the wild remnants were also reclaimed; first the area around Stolwijk, later on around Achterbroek and Berkenwoude. These reclamations did not develop from the outer dikes, like the older ones, but in two directions from canals in the polder that were used for transportation. Typical remnants from these younger reclamations are the ribbon-like occupation axes on both sides of these watercourses. The ribbon-shaped plots of land sometimes had a fixed length (for example, in the Vlist polder and along the Lek between Bergambacht and Schoonhoven). In other areas, the plots are very long, up to several kilometres, such as near Ouderkerk. Isolated settlements also occur on the *donken*.

Flora and fauna

The Krimpenerwaard plant and animal communities are of great value (Natuurwetenschappelijke Commissie 1986). They are inextricably linked with its reclamation history, water management and agricultural use, and thus the landscape structure (Heidemij 1985, PPD Zuid-Holland 1985). After reclamation of the marsh woodland the original flora and fauna were replaced by species of open and wet cultural landscapes. As a result of the restricted and only superficial drainage of the land, a gradient of land-use intensity developed. Those parts of the land plots close to the farms were used more intensively than the sites far away, which resulted in a clear biotic gradient between the borders and the centre of the polder. For many centuries most of the land was used principally for haymaking. Only along the River Lek, between Lekkerkerk and Ammerstol and near Stolwijk, relatively intensive flax and hemp cultures occurred till the end of the nineteenth century. The land in the centre of the polder was practically never manured and only used to the extent that a nutrient-poor, but botanically rich, fen-meadow vegetation developed. As a result of recent lowering of water levels and manuring, the majority of these rich vegetation units have disappeared. In some nature reserves near Berkenwoude and Gouderak there are still some remnants of them present. In the Nooitgedacht nature reserve specific measures have been taken to safeguard the internationally very rare marsh-marigold hayfields (Beckers 2000). The former differences in land-use intensities are nowadays still recognizable in the vegetation of the sides of ditches and grasslands. Old peat-cuttings have in some places created water-filled pits in which valuable aquatic and semi-terrestial natural vegetation types develop. Some of these pits are used as duck decoys and, because they are situated in inaccessible quiet areas in the centre of the polder, they form important rest and breeding areas for birds such as kestrel, long-eared owl and tawny owl (Weidema *et al.* 1976). The numerous small bushes and marshes spread all over the polder hold breeding populations of song-birds and birds of prey and the rough meadows are important breeding areas for meadow birds. In autumn and winter the Krimpenerwaard is occupied by thousands of migratory birds and winter visitors that forage and rest there.

Water management

The Krimpenerwaard is an example of a peat polder with shallow ground-water. The water level in the waterways is very high, ranging from 30 to 60 cm below the land surface. The peatland is a complete unity with the water; it is completely saturated and in some places more or less floating. Excess water is channelled through an extensive network of drainage canals and ditches to pumping stations, from where it is pumped up and out into the surrounding rivers. Water table management is not optimal because of the ageing of the pumping stations, and the poor spatial distribution of them and the drainage network. In these areas small differences of centimetres may have massive impacts on the total water balance (cf. Moning & Naberman 1998). The total area of open water is large and its quality is very important for both agriculture and nature. Nevertheless, the water quality is rather poor practically everywhere, because in summer Rhine water polluted with nitrates, phosphates and heavy metals is pumped in for agricultural purposes, and in autumn and winter, in particular, a high percentage of farm manure leaks to ground and surface waters; also until four or five years ago household water from occupation areas was still drained into the surface waters. As a result, in a considerable part of the polder, the formerly species-rich water and ditch-side vegetation has disappeared and has been replaced by eutrophic species. The introduction of polluted river water may seem counterproductive, but as it is of better quality than the water in the polder itself, as far as nutrients and oxygen are concerned, the polder ditches are at least kept viable.

Recreation

In the Krimpenerwaard various forms of open-air recreation such as walking, cycling, skating, canoeing, fishing and camping can be encountered, although most of them at a low level. The largest recreation pressure is found near the population areas in the south-west and close to Gouda. Increasing numbers of cyclists come from the nearby large cities. On the rivers there are various forms of water recreation and a number of river banks are used for sunbathing and fishing. Close to Bergambacht some small beaches are situated along the River Lek, and fishing facilities have been constructed. The watercourses and the River Vlist are used for rowing and canoeing, but the many dams limit the possibilities. As in other Dutch polders, skating in winter is the most prominent form of recreation. There are some signposted paths for tours that last one to two days, and two international long-distance paths cross the area. Although there are at least six campsites, the overall recreation pressure on the Krimpenerwaard is not very high.

Threats and their proposed resolutions

The biggest environmental threats to the Krimpenerwaard landscape are the continued lowering of groundwater levels, the enrichment of water and soils, and the pollution of the bottom sediments of watercourses and ponds. In addition, until recently the filling of ditches and ponds, the metalling of farmyards, the transformation from 'fairway polder' to 'traffic by road polder', the construction of large roads, and extensions of built-up areas have also had severe landscape impacts.

The recently adopted rural development plan for 10,000 ha of agricultural land, whose initial phases go back to 1982, favours nature as an integrated part of rural development. In the commission that made the plan, municipalities, polder-boards, NGOs for nature conservation, and organizations of farmers and of recreation enterprises were all represented. They had to deal with a severe agriculture–nature conflict from the beginning of the planning procedure. The debate centred on two points in particular: the management of the water table (lowering for agriculture versus raising for nature), and the extent of the land to be set aside for nature conservation and 'new' nature.

As a consequence of government policy reports – the Nature Policy Plan and the Structure Plan for the Rural Areas – research has been carried out in the Krimpenerwaard on how to translate the concept of sustainability into specific measures for the area. Various alternatives for nature development have been elaborated, specifically focusing on marshy woodlands, peat bogs, semi-natural grasslands and lightly used grasslands (Den Held 1990). Specific goals for these ecosystems include the establishment of new marshy woodlands and peat bogs, together with the restoration of semi-natural and lightly used grasslands and well-developed bank vegetation by adapted agricultural management.

The new integrated landscape development plan projects the establishment of nature conservation areas of more than 30 per cent of the total area of the Krimpenerwaard! The plan envisages the development of marshy woodlands on the peat-clay gradient and of nutrient-poor grasslands and nature reserves in areas with upward seepage. Several measures will be taken in order to facilitate this by creating poorer and wetter habitat conditions. There will be separation of the water systems of 'natural' and agricultural areas, with less drainage and higher water tables in the former, anti-eutrofication measures, and the cutting of turf from at least 350 ha, causing impoverishment of the surface soil and shallower ground waters. Apart from this, the management of nature by farmers on at least 2000 ha is to be stimulated with substantial incentives, the intention being to establish so-called 'ecological zones' along watercourses. Habitat for meadow bird species and the quality of the vegetation at the sides of ditches and grasslands will be priorities. The agricultural development is directed towards achieving farm sizes of 30 to 40 ha with convenient parcelling of land and modern box stalls for stock. The location of nature reserves should not limit unduly the prospects of continued, long-term dairy farming. A water table lowering to 60 cm is foreseen in all areas with a structure that is good from an agricultural point of view (c. 3750 ha). The elongated plots in this area will be shortened and will get better access.

Nature development in these areas of The Netherlands depends upon management agreements between government and farmers. Farmers or associations of farmers are paid for: landscape management such as coppicing, pollarding, and management of ditch sides, ponds, marshes, reed areas, dykes, and the cleaning of waterways; the establishment of landscape elements such as woods, border plantations and ponds; and postponed mowing to favour meadow-birds, the protection of nests and restricted fertilizing. In the near future it is intended that the management measures themselves will not be the base for financial compensation but the nature 'results' will be. The measures for a specific region are progressively elaborated in 'enterprise nature plans' of associations of farmers, a development that is strongly encouraged by officials. This output-oriented approach fits perfectly with the output-oriented increased production of certified products with a strong regional identity, such as cheese and lamb.

Water management is crucial for the futures of both agriculture and nature. Recently a new, integrated water management approach was introduced as part of the integrated development plan. It comprises a flexible water level management policy with less river water input, increased buffering of rain water by deepening of ditches and canals, the broadening of the main canals and the acceptance of high-water levels due to precipitation in summer. In addition it envisages: the building of new pumping stations, a new system of internal reservoirs for superfluous polder-water, segregation of water systems of 'natural' areas from the surroundings, several anti-eutrofication measures involving improved sewage purification, fine-tuned manuring and no manuring of ditch sides, all houses connected to the sewage drainage system, deep dredging of polluted underwater sediments of canals and ditches, and the removal of duck-weed from canals and ditches (Moning & Naberman 1998).

The region will increasingly provide recreation for nearby urban societies. Recently the Province of South-Holland decided to make new bicycle paths, to open some more quays for walking and to link the long-distance path from Krimpenerwaard to Lopikerwaard.

The integrated final plan for the Krimpenerwaard was developed from separate agricultural and environmental models. Each sector was studied to find points of agreement and conflict between the two interest groups. The final judgement was based on cost–benefit analyses of each situation, the suitability of the sector's size and its manageability for sustainable land use, the possibility for integrating nature management into farming operations, and the feasibility of sustainable development of the environment, nature and agriculture.

Box 1

Japanese landscapes

T. Shigematsu and Y. Yamamori

Japan is a very mountainous country with much of its farming confined to the coastal flatlands, or to terraces carved into the hills and valleys. Mountain areas were once cut and burned partially or extensively to provide grass forage, and sometimes grazing for stock, but have now been extensively abandoned or reforested for timber production and flood protection. Forest cover in Japan is about 70 per cent, compared to 10 per cent in Britain, or 30 per cent in France. Unusual extensive *Miscanthus* spp. grasslands, pink in the summer with the flowers of *Rhododendron kiusianum*, still survive in and around the great outer caldera of Mt. Aso in Kyushu, grazed by tan-coloured cattle. Imports of cheap beef from Australia and New Zealand threaten the local economy and between 1955 and 1989 farmhouses declined from 10,000 to 4000. Ways are being sought to keep farmers on the land by exploiting income from the great numbers of tourists who visit the Mt. Aso National Park.

Terraced rice paddies are ancient, beautiful and species-rich landscapes all over Japan, but their upkeep is very labour-intensive, and in many places they are being abandoned as the profitability of farming declines, despite big subsidies. Sometimes, as in the Hoshino village of the Fukuoka Prefecture, other uses, such as tree nurseries, are being found for the terraces, now often repaired with concrete rather than stone to the detriment of the vernacular architecture. The surrounding lands, once exploited for coppice, forage, hunting wild boar and the gathering of berries and mushrooms, are reverting to conifer plantations. Richer lowland rice paddies are also subject to change. Those of the Koto Plain in the Shiga Prefecture were laid out in the eighth century with the Jori grid system of a 110 x 110 m major grid, subdivided into 110 x 10 m plots, producing sufficient to feed a person for a year. The paddies are intersected by watercourses with willow-lined banks and beautiful nucleated settlements. Modernization and rebuilding of houses, roads and the water supply system, together with industrial development, all threaten the traditional landscape. Better planning control and more support for the farmers are needed if it is to survive.

Vast sand dunes, derived from both the sea and alluvial fans eroded from the steep mountains, fringe large parts of the Japanese coast. Behind them brackish and freshwater lagoons have been converted to rice paddies protected from the sea and encroaching sand by natural pine forest and by afforestation of the dunes. Some of these forests, such as the Niji-no-Matsubara (Rainbow Pine Beach) of the Saga Prefecture, are of great ecological value with stands and veteran trees of *Pinus thunbergii* and *P. densiflora, and Cryptomeria japonica, Chamaecyparis obtusa* and *C. pisifera* plantations. Here and elsewhere, for example at Kameda-go and Toyano-gata lagoon near Niigata city, the paddies inland are having their watercourses canalized and concreted, and the development of golf courses, resort complexes, roads and industry threaten the integrity of the coastal landscapes through tree felling and drainage.

Box 2

Ejin Oasis, Inner Mongolia, China

Chen Changdu

Surrounded by the sandy and shrubby deserts of the Gobi, the Ejin Oasis lies at the western end of the Alxa Plateau on the flat alluvial plain of the lower reaches and delta of the Ruo Shui. The natural vegetation consists mainly of riparian forests of *Populus euphratica* and Russian olive (*Elaeagnus angustifolia*), shrublands of *Tamarix* spp. and meadow communities of *Phragmites communis, Sophora alopecuroides* and *Achnatherum splendens*. Although the climate is extremely arid, the soil moisture has enabled the development of irrigated agriculture with crop fields, rangelands, settlements and a town going back to the Han Dynasty (206BC – 220AD). Outside the oasis livestock husbandry predominates. On the rangelands the main stock are goats and camels. The main crop is spring wheat, with corn, sorghum, highland barley and millet also being cultivated. The attractive scenery, combined with historic monuments, especially the ruins of the Black City of the Western Xia Regime (1038–1227), and cool summer climate make this a well-kown tourist destination. The poplar and Russian olive forests are Tertiary relicts and biologically very rich. The whole area is of archaeological importance.

A nature reserve helps protect the area, but needs enlargement. Even then it would not address the fundamental problem which threatens the survival of the oasis, namely a reduction in the flow of the Ruo Shui which is lowering the ground water table. Large tracts of the forests are withering with a loss of their biodiversity, the crop fields are shrinking in extent and there is a shortage of drinking water for people and livestock. As a result the population is gradually migrating away from the oasis. The key to countering these damaging trends is more water and the need to transfer it from the middle reaches to the lower reaches of the Ruo Shui at the right time of the year, that is, when it is required during the growing season.

Mountains

Throughout the world the landscapes of mountain areas, maintained as open pasture and meadow by livestock husbandry, are among the richest in wildlife and most cherished for open-air recreation. But they are also among the most threatened. The traditional farming systems provide little financial reward and are a very hard way of life, which young people are increasingly unprepared to take on. If the landscapes are abandoned a return to forest is inevitable and this process is advanced in many areas. Finding ways to support communities by helping old ways of life and by developing new ones is not easy.

Chapter 5
Sognefjord, Norway

I. Austad and L. Hauge

Introduction

The Sognefjord is unique. It is the deepest fjord in the world and the second longest, with steep climate gradients from coastal to inland districts and from sea level to the mountains. The climate is influenced by Norway's largest glacier (Jostedalsbreen). Thus there is great variation in natural conditions within a relatively limited area and vegetation types include thermophilic deciduous woodland, coastal heathland and alpine vegetation. The Sognefjord is a typical Norwegian fjord landscape dominated by natural elements such as fjord arms, steep high mountains, screes, canyons, glaciers, rivers, deltas and waterfalls. Great contrasts over short distances are characteristic of the fjord landscape where the mountain-sides rise directly from the fjord to an altitude of 1300–1500 m. The highest mountain in the area is Store Skagastolstind in Jotunheimen (2403 m). The Sognefjord reaches a maximum depth of 1309 m. The area is defined by the 12 municipalities that surround the Sognefjord today: Solund, Gulen, Hyllestad, Hoyanger, Balestrand, Vik, Leikanger, Sogndal, Luster, Aurland, Aardal and Laerdal and covers 10,689 km².

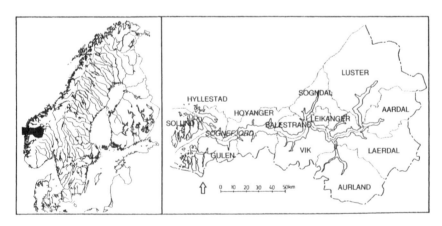

5.1 Sognefjord, Norway

Geology and topography

The bedrock consists mainly of Precambrian basement rocks (granites and granitic gneisses) which are poor in nutrients and weather slowly (Kvale 1980). In some areas, phyllite, a rich Cambro-Silurian rock, weathers to give a fairly fertile soil. In the most westerly part of the area Devonian conglomerate is the dominant rock. The steep hill and mountain-sides are affected by scree activity and abundant seepage water, which can result in good mineral supplies locally. The topography clearly shows the effects of glacial activity (Aarseth 1989). Originally, most valleys had a typical U-shaped profile with distinct glacial cirques. In the lower parts they can develop a V-form emphasized by small waterfalls. The valley bottoms may also be flat, especially in the inland regions. The soil mostly consists of minerogenous material, such as moraine, scree and glaci-fluvial deposits. Marine deposits are found in the former fjord bottoms, up to 130 metres in Luster. At higher altitudes and in the mountains, the soils consist mainly of thin till, talus and scree material in combination with exposed bedrock, peat and bog (Klakegg *et al.* 1989). In the coastal areas, where precipitation is high, podsols are common. In the fjord regions, brown humus-rich soil may develop.

Most of the valleys open directly into the deep, narrow arms of the Sognefjord between steep mountain-sides, but there are some hanging tributary valleys. Many of the valleys are today influenced by tongues of the glacier. The inner parts of the fjord are characterized by alpine landforms and the Jostedalsbreen glacier, and the rivers are short and steep with many waterfalls. More rounded landforms are typical of the coastal zone. The agrarian landscape is characterized by small-scale variation and forms a mosaic including considerable amounts of bare rock, forests, forest edges, hedgerows and solitary trees, resulting in a great diversity of plant communities and ecological processes. Cultivated land is concentrated along the fjord and at the mouths of the valleys.

Vegetation

The great variation in geology, topography and local climate result in a highly varied, complex natural vegetation. The vegetation is a mixture of natural coniferous and deciduous forests (*Pinus sylvestris, Betula pendula/B. pubescens*), spruce plantations (mainly *Picea abies*), coppiced and pollarded woodlands (*Corylus avellana, Ulmus glabra, Fraxinus excelsior, Tilia cordata and Betula* sp.), wooded pastures/groves, open pastures, hay meadows and wooded hay meadows, wetlands and mires, river deltas and seashore meadows, heathlands and alpine vegetation. The lowlands belong to the southern boreal zone (Dahl *et al.* 1986), but the steep montain-sides result in a rather sharp zonation through middle and northern boreal and alpine zones over short distances. The fjord zone and the lowest parts of the valleys are characterized by stands of rich deciduous forests with nutrient-rich soil. In the middle boreal zone, including the upper valley bottoms, mixed woods of *Betula pubescens* and *Alnus incana* dominate. *Alnus incana* woods are common on unstable soils with ample seepage water and in alluvial zones along river banks and deltas. *Betula pubescens* woodland dominates the natural vegetation at higher altitudes towards the tree line and penetrates towards the lowlands in cool, shaded parts of the valleys. Near the coast *Calluna vulgaris* heathlands are a typical feature. The tree limit varies from 600 m along the coast up to 1200 m in inner Sogn. Above the tree limit, large mire complexes and poor oligotrophic plant communities are important elements.

Animal populations

The fauna is varied, reflecting wide variations in natural conditions. Red deer are common in the lowlands along the fjord and near the coast. Their numbers are increasing. Reindeer are typical in the mountain areas in the inner and middle Sogn. Moose have been seen in the eastern part. Hare, fox, willow grouse, ptarmigan and black grouse are hunted. Woodpeckers and bats are common in the traditional cultural landscape. At the coast there are seabirds of many species and the deltas and wetlands are important feeding grounds for migrating birds. In the sea porpoises and seals can be seen. Salmon are common in the lower parts of the rivers, especially in the inner Sogn. The lakes and rivers in the mountains hold stocks of trout and char.

Land use

The cultural landscape in the Sognefjord region can be divided into four main types: the coastal strip, the fjord districts, the valleys and lowland plains, and the mountain areas. The natural resources have been utilized for many generations, and distinct human-dependent vegetation types have developed. This is a result of the interplay and mutual dependence between natural conditions and farming methods adapted to them, of which fire, grazing, lopping and hay-making are the most important. Thus the vegetation is very heterogeneous and reflects also differences in cultural-historical background and management techniques (Austad, Hauge & Helle 1993, 1994).

Both in the western coastal areas and in the mountain areas, there are traces of settlement dating back to 6000–5000 BC. However, no stone carvings have been found along the Sognefjord. Stone constructions such as tombs are typical features of the area, and date back to the Bronze Age (1000–500 BC.). In about 500 BC the climate turned cooler. The Black Death in AD 1349–50 had a devastating effect on the population. Dry-stone walls, piles of stones cleared from arable land, carefully constructed roads, bridges, irrigation channels, ditches and remnants of old buildings are valuable and important historical artefacts.

Various types of historical buildings have been noted in the region. Most important and best known are the stave churches, which were built in the period between AD 1150 and 1250. Five stave churches still standing today are at Borgund (Laerdal), Kaupanger (Sogndal), Umes (Luster), Undredal (Aurland) and Hopperstad (Vik). Old stone churches can be seen in Luster, Balestrand and Vik. In several places there are impressive winding roads. Apart from this, farm buildings in the local style and traditional cluster-type and linear farms can be seen in their natural surroundings, both in the mountain areas and in the lowlands. The small cotters' farms, which illustrate how maximum use was made of scarce natural resources, are also typical. Villages, mainly seashore settlements dominated by small wooden houses in the traditional style, are common. Laerdalsoyi (Laerdal) is the best preserved village of this type in the region. Along the coast there are still small fishing communities (*fiskevaer*), of which Utvaer (Solund) is a good example. These are visible evidence of the all-round use that earlier generations made of marine resources.

In a country with a long non-productive winter season such as in Norway, the population had to store provisions for lean periods. Large quantities of fodder (grass, heather and leaves) were required to supplement the food supply of domestic animals (Austad 1988). Burning and clearing land for farming, improving and fencing off arable land and pasture, and developing irrigation systems were typical activities. Fuel (wood and peat) had to be collected and forests logged. The actual species of animals domesticated or plants cultivated and the harvesting techniques used varied during the history of the region.

Grain production and, from the end of the seventeenth century, potatoes, combined with dairy and sheep husbandry, were the dominant types of farming. Hunting and fishing also played an important role in the farm economy. The outfields, including mountains, were used for grazing and hay-making, and for collecting firewood, materials and timber for households, and fodder for domestic animals by pollarding and coppicing. Along the coast heathlands formed as a result of fire and grazing. Exploitation of mires for peat was common both near the coast and in the mountains. The use of juniper trunks for poles and posts was very important (Austad & Hauge 1990).

Although natural conditions and therefore the cultural background and landscape types in Norway are very different from those in many other countries in temperate and tropical regions, there are many similarities in the ways in which natural resources have been exploited. Many of the old structures in the landscape can be seen, and traditional agricultural techniques are still in use, maintaining authentic examples of various human-influenced vegetation types.

The modern rural economy

Since the Second World War, farming has been modernized and intensified, and agricultural practices have changed as a result. Decreasing numbers of domestic animals, a growing area of spruce plantations and the conversion of pastures and hay meadows into woodlands are typical developments today. Large-scale production of fruit (apples, pears, plums, cherries, raspberries, strawberries) and vegetables (cabbage, carrots, turnips) has become more important. Originally dominated by farming activity and fishing combined with some hunting, gradual development towards clusters of seashore settlements and small commercial and industrial towns has taken place. With a few exceptions the land is private, and one-family properties dominate most of the area. The farms are relatively small with an infield area of 5–10 ha and larger outfields. In the mountain areas the rights of ownership (grazing, hunting, fishing) may be shared between many farmers. Some areas in the fjord region are protected as national parks or nature reserves.

Income from hunting red deer and salmon fishing rights in the fjord and rivers are important to some farmers. Fishing still plays an important role, especially the commercial sprat fishery. Trout fishing in small lakes in the mountains is of less economic importance. In earlier times the picking of hazel nuts used to be important. People are free to pick wild berries (*Vaccinium myrtillus, V. vitis-idaea, Rubus chamaemorus*) and mushrooms except in in-field areas. Wild berries are not picked on a commercial basis in the area. Agricultural production is now concentrated in areas where mechanized agricultural techniques are efficient. Large parts of the outfields, even highly productive areas, have fallen into disuse. However, many traditional farming techniques, such as lopping, hay-making (scything) and grazing, are still in active use (Austad *et al.* 1991). Forestry is important, especially in the central and inner part of the region. The Scots pine (*Pinus sylvestris*) is common and covers large areas. Spruce trees (mainly *Picea abies*) are being planted for the pulp industry. Traditional harvesting techniques such as pollarding are still practised at some farms to allow the collection of leaves, twigs or branches for animal fodder. The former widespread use of young shoots for various tools and for making baskets and barrel hoops has come to an end.

During the last hundred years, the energy of some of the waterfalls has been harnessed in hydro-electric power plants and used in the aluminium industry in Sogn (Aardal and Hoyanger). Ship-building was important in Hyllestad and Solund. However, the main industry is still agriculture, with aquaculture and tourism growing in importance.

Settlement and transport

Approximately 40,000 people live in the Sognefjord area. The municipality of Aardal has the highest population (about 7000 inhabitants). Some of the municipalities have experienced a decrease in population since the Second World War. The proportion of elderly people is also showing a tendency to rise in most of the municipalities. Most people live along the fjord and in the lowland valleys. In general, villages are situated where rivers run into the fjord. Some of these are old seashore settlements. Throughout history, the sea (fjord) has been the main route for transport and communications for people living in the area. Important trade routes between Bergen and Oslo made use of the fjord. Along the coast there were well-defined fairways and trade routes between Bergen and Trondheim and to the fishing banks. Today express boats and ferries use the fjord. Ferries are still a very important part of the communication system, linking together the surrounding municipalities. A network of roads follows the fjord and the valley bottoms and crosses the mountains in a few places. Tunnels link the remotest valleys with the rest of the region. Some of the mountain passes are closed during the winter. There are regular flights to other parts of the county and to Oslo and Bergen from Sogndal airport.

Recreation

The tourist industry is very important in the area and plays a major part in the economy. Many cruise ships call in at the Sognefjord during the summer season. Cultural monuments and the impressive natural surroundings are important assets for the tourist industry. The traditional cultural landscape clearly illustrates the interplay between man and nature and the contrasts between man-made structures and natural forces. The mountain areas (and some glaciers) are used for walking in summer. Caravanning is becoming increasingly popular. With the growing efforts being made to promote tourism, especially in rural areas, the management of cultural monuments and traditional cultural landscapes and arrangements for public access will become important. The local population also enjoys opportunities for a wide range of different activities, such as walking, skiing, camping, hunting, fishing and picking berries.

Cultural associations

Special elements of the cultural landscape and the interplay between people and their surroundings have attracted many artists to the area. Nikolai Astrup (1880–1928) and Theodor Kittelsen (1857–1914) were particularly fascinated by the mystique associated with forms such as sculptural pollarded trees. The natural and cultural landscape also inspired many painters in the 'golden age' of national romanticism, who painted people and farmsteads against the background of the dramatic fjord landscape. They included painters such as Johan Christian Dahl (1788–1857), Adolph Tidemand (1854–1891), Hans Fredrik Gude (1825–1903) and Johannes Flintoe (1787–1870). Henrik Sorensen (1882–1962) also found inspiration in the area.

The regional variant of the traditional Norwegian costume is called the *Sognebunad*. Both male and female costumes are decorated with jewellery and silver accessories. The *bunad* can always be worn on formal occasions. It is timeless and has been passed on from generation to generation. Originally a *bunad* from a particular district was worn only by a person born and bred there and the costume matched the dialect of the wearer. Historical dramas have been performed at historical sites.

The importance of the landscape

As a result of the wide gradients in climate, topography, geology and cultural history, the vegetation in the Sognefjord area has a high biological diversity. The herb-rich hay meadows are among the most valuable and vulnerable plant communities in the traditional cultural landscape. The mosaic structure ensures a broad range of important habitats for plants, small mammals, insects and reptiles. The scenery is magnificent, underlined by strong contrasts. Many semi-natural vegetation types are also valuable recreation areas.

Trends threatening the landscape

The managed vegetation types are part of Norway's cultural heritage and can only be protected through traditional management techniques. It is essential to hand down knowledge of traditional farming skills in order to maintain ecological processes and the biological diversity and quality of the landscape. Traditional cultural landscapes with a variety of semi-natural vegetation types are unstable ecosystems, entirely dependent upon active, traditional use for their survival. If such use is discontinued, their characteristic appearance is lost. Fewer and fewer farmers still master the various old techniques. Today disused outfields are becoming overgrown with woodland, or are being planted with spruce trees, cultivated or developed in other ways, thus threatening many habitat types and species.

Some of the threats and problems facing marginal agricultural land in hilly and mountainous areas and in outlying districts far from markets are common to different regions and countries. In such areas the restructuring of agriculture and political decisions have made agriculture less profitable, and depopulation results. Land use becomes extensive rather than intensive, arable land is used as hayfield, hayfield as pasture and so on. Finally, the land is left fallow and becomes overgrown. On the other hand, modern farming practices, involving putting land under intensive production, more use of fertilizer on meadows, and a greater use of herbicides and pesticides on raspberries and other fruit are even more damaging to wildlife and amenity. The steep topography of the Sognefjord area means that there may be a substantial run-off of nutrients. More intensive forestry, which also involves the construction of many roads in steep terrain, has led to erosion in some places. Changes in animal husbandry, for instance the reduction in number of animals grazing at farms, do not only affect the vegetation, but also the way buildings are used, older ones often falling into disrepair. Summer farms are often used as holiday homes, and may be rebuilt and redecorated using new materials and colours that break with local tradition. Similar developments are taking place along the coast, where small, old seashore and fishing communities are being transformed into holiday resorts, leaving many old structures and buildings to fall into disrepair, while the heathlands are ungrazed and become overgrown.

Fish farming is a growth industry along the coast, and can entail various types of conflict arising from, for example, changes in the genetic make-up of salmon, the use of pesticides, pollution from intensive feeding, restrictions on public access, and unsightly buildings. Careful planning and adequate restrictions are needed to avoid unwanted developments. Commercial kelp harvesting also has negative effects on coastal ecosystems.

The abandonment of cultural landscapes generally results in a decrease in biodiversity. Both species and ecologically diverse semi-natural vegetation types are being lost. Heathlands are threatened by development, spruce planting and the effects of acid rain. Valuable traditional landscape elements have fallen into disuse and are under great pressure from other forms of land use. Small farms do not provide an adequate income, thus forcing the farmers to combine agriculture with other jobs. Abandonment and/or depopulation are typical trends. Traditionally managed cultural landscapes are unfortunately not considered to be sufficiently intensive production systems. Farmers have not so far received sufficient financial support to survive on such marginal farms. Adjustments to GATT and OECD rules and harmonization with the EU result in more and more standardized production throughout the country. Agricultural policy favours large, mechanized holdings.

The future

Some of these undesirable trends can be countered by protective designations. Valuable cultural landscapes can be designated as 'Landscape Protection Areas' which allow most forms of traditional management to be maintained. So far, however, very few strategies for conserving such cultural landscapes have been developed within, or outside, designated areas. A more generally accepted objective is to maintain a viable, active agricultural sector which meets environmental standards, takes into account the cultural history and ecological processes that ensure a rich flora and fauna, maintains the aesthetic qualities of the landscape, and protects cultural monuments and the Norwegian cultural heritage, without fossilizing change and being museum-like. To achieve this co-operation between authorities at local, regional and national level is essential. The Ministry of Agriculture must develop economic instruments that can be used to maintain valuable cultural landscapes on a larger scale than today. Currently, farmers may apply for supplements for the management of traditional semi-natural vegetation types on a small scale. Such supplements are also granted on condition that the farmer himself supplies a substantial amount of unpaid labour in the area.

Our knowledge of management strategies for cultural landscapes needs to be improved at all levels. Research concerning appropriate management techniques needs priority. Plans for the protection, management, provision of funds and development of agriculture, recreation, and tourism must be drawn up in collaboration with farmers. Supplements should be granted for management at yearly or longer intervals for restoration purposes. In addition support may be provided for measures to improve or ensure public access to such areas, as well as for special measures to do with fencing, gates and information.

A number of research projects concerning traditional cultural landscapes and semi-natural vegetation types organized by Sogn og Fjordane College have been carried out in the region (Austad 1988, Austad & Hauge 1989, 1990, Austad & Skogen 1990, Austad *et al.* 1991, Austad, Hauge & Skogen in prep., Hauge 1988). The cultural landscape of all 26 municipalities in Sogn og Fjordane county was registered in the cross-sectoral project 'Maintenance and conservation of the cultural landscape in Sogn og Fjordane, Norway' (Austad, Hauge & Helle, 1993, 1994). A project concerning changes in biological diversity in traditional wooded hay meadows and wooded pastures when management regimes are discontinued and/or drastically altered, financed by the Research Council of Norway, is nearing completion (Austad & Losvik 1998, Hauge 1998, Moe & Botnen 1997).

Box 3

Mount Carmel, Israel

D.Y. Kaplan

Mount Carmel lies in the northern section of the coastal area of Israel and represents a typical semi-natural Mediterranean landscape with outstanding biological, cultural and landscape diversity and scenic features. The landscape is biologically highly diverse with close to 1500 vascular plant species in open grasslands, batha, oak (*Quercus calliprinos*) maquis, pine (*Pinus halepensis*) forest and oak (*Q. ithaburensis*) park forest. Archaeological evidence of continuous human activities can be found beginning with late Middle Pleistocene remains at the world famous cave of Carmel, Neanderthal and *Paleoantropos palaestinensis* humans and with subsequent continued human occupation till the present.

Of the total area of 232 km², 84 km² have been declared a national park which incorporates nature reserves of 31 km² and a wildlife reintroduction sanctuary. Pine plantations, open-door recreation areas, and traditional and modern agropastoral exploitation are the main land uses (Shorer 1983, Naveh 1990). The park is bordered by the metropolis of Haifa, and in its centre are located two Druze villages. With this location Mount Carmel is the most important recreation attraction in the heavily populated coastal area of Israel, visited by more than two million people annually. The most important landscape threats to which the Carmel is exposed are:

* urban development of the Haifa metropolis, sprawling into the park;
* industrial development in Haifa Bay with increased demonstrated effects of air pollutants on the ecosystem;
* increasing pressure of visitors, disproportional to the existing recreation facilities;
* destructive wild fires; and
* abandonment of traditional agriculture and pastoral use of the land followed by brush encroachment.

In order to relieve these threats and to ensure co-ordinated and integrated conservation management of Mount Carmel as a whole, a biosphere reserve plan is now in preparation by the Nature Reserves Authority of Israel, supported by the German Environment Ministry.

References

Naveh, Z. (1990) 'Proposal for a pilot test for the preparation of redbooks on threatened Mediterranean landscapes in Italy and Israel'. Submitted to the MEDSPA Program 1991.
Shorer, J. (ed.) (1983) *Mount Carmel – Man and Landscape*, Society for the Protection of Nature, Israel (in Hebrew).

Box 4

Atlantic heathland, Ytre Fensfjord and Lurefjorden, Norway

P. Kaland

Open, treeless heathlands of dwarf, ericaceous shrubs, principally heather (*Calluna vulgaris*), have covered vast tracts of infertile acid soils of the oceanic zone of north-west Europe for at least the last 4000 years. They are the product of infield–outfield farming systems, which still survive in parts of Norway where farming was traditionally combined with fishing and hunting for seabirds, seals and whales. In the mild oceanic climate sheep were grazed on the heathlands throughout the year; cattle were overwintered indoors, fed on grass, heather and other fodder. The heaths were burnt from time to time to rejuvenate old woody heather and provide nutritious young growth. Dung, seaweed, refuse, turves, and peat from the bogs which fill depressions in the landscape were used to fertilize the infields cropped with oats, barley and potatoes, or cut for hay.

Although of low plant and animal diversity, many of the heather species and insects and birds characteristic of these heathlands rarely occur elsewhere. In late summer the terrain is carpeted purple with the flowering heather, but it can be dark and foreboding for much of the year. Stone farmhouses, built in the longhouse style which goes back to prehistoric times, are scattered in isolated farms; more recent houses are mainly along the roads built in the last century. Remains of mesolithic hunter/fisher 'strandlooping' culture dwellings up to 9000 years old occur along the shorelines and show these cultures turning to farming and moving inland to clear the forest 4000–5000 years ago.

In the last fifty years farming has been modernized and intensified on the better land, while poor and remote farmland has been abandoned. In the absence of grazing, mowing and burning, the heathland is becoming overgrown with shrubs and trees. In many places old farmlands have been afforested with spruce. To maintain the threatened heathlands the practical knowledge of traditional land-use methods still held by older farmers is being exploited through the establishment of a National Heathland Centre. This is reintroducing the old systems and stock and helping to market them as ecological products. It will also promote education, recreation and tourism in the area which is designated as a Landscape Reserve of the Norwegian Ministry of Environment.

Mediterranean islands

Cut off by the sea, island landscapes and their inhabitants are often very different from their mainland counterparts. Their isolation shields the populations of those few species that manage to reach them from competitors raised in the harder school of continental competition, leading to the evolution of unique island forms. Human settlement, founded frequently from eclectic sources, often leads to distinctive cultures and landscapes. The hardships of island life are perhaps even greater than those of the mountains, and, like them, depopulation is a major problem. Crete exhibits many of these characteristics, and its offshore island Gávdhos even more.

Chapter 6
Gávdhos, Crete

A.T. Grove, J. Moody and O. Rackham

Introduction

The Greek island of Gávdhos, 40 km south of Crete, has a unique landscape which is threatened by abandonment, destructive fires and potential tourist development (Fig. 6.1).

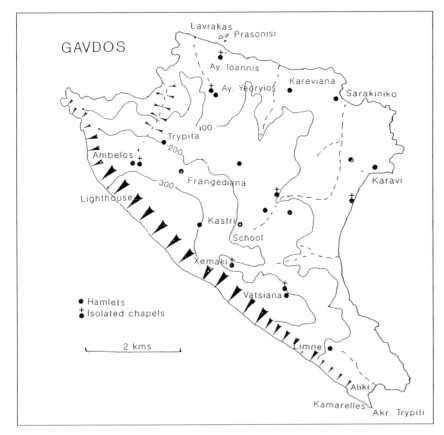

6.1 Map of Gávdhos

The southernmost outpost of Europe, Gávdhos is a world of its own; it is not just a detached part of Crete. It is a land of soft rocks, dunes, indurated blown sand, calcrete caprock and tremendous gullies. It has plant communities unknown elsewhere in the world, square kilometres of archaeological sites, a distinctive vernacular architecture, and a way of life that dates back several hundred years. It is this combination that makes it such an unusual and special place. Gávdhos has so far entirely escaped the ravages of bulldozing, un-planned building, and over-intensified agriculture. However, other problems that affect Crete appear in an extreme form on this lonely islet. In the seventeenth century it came within an inch of succumbing to piracy; now it is threatened by depopulation. As every serious visitor to Gávdhos knows, it is hard to get to, and can be exceedingly hard to get away from. It is surrounded by stormy seas, and one cannot land if there is any east in the wind. In winter it may be unapproachable for weeks on end. Such isolation is the main reason given for its declining population.

The island of Gávdhos is situated to the south of Crete (latitude 34° 50' N, longitude 24° 05' E). It has an area of 32 square kilometres. The island is a township (*koinótis*) in the district of Sélinon and province of Khania, Crete. The land is owned by a large number of present and former inhabitants. There is apparently no common land. The Greek Forestry Department might lay claim to part of the island on the grounds that it has become overgrown with trees.

The structure of the landscape

The island is mountainous, though less so than Crete. From the low north coast it rises in gentle undulations – broken by hidden ravines and gullies – to a high limestone ridge, reaching 345 m above sea level. From here a wall of cliff plunges into the sea on the south-west side, to one of the most beautiful and wild beaches in Crete. The south tip, called Kamarelles ('Little Arches') or Cape Trypiu ('Holed'), is a spine of rock pierced by three natural arches, a fittingly dramatic end to Europe.

The backbone of the island is a ridge of hard limestone containing karst depressions. On this limestone, there is little active erosion, except for a few terraces which have lost some soil. Flysch deposits, composed of bright red and green shales and green sandstones, are associated with the hard limestones. There has been some igneous activity in the north-east part of the island; although there are no volcanic rocks, flysch and other materials have been highly metamorphosed into glittery mica-schists and serpentines. The north-east half of the island is mostly made up of Neogene deposits of interbedded clays, marls, and sandstones.

The north coast is covered in sand-dunes, which extend well inland; they are among the best examples in Crete of such landscapes. Some of the dunes have been partially stabilized by vegetation. Old sand-dunes, shaped by northerly winds, have been cemented to form a sandstone rock (aeolianite). They are extensively developed up to 200 m and more in altitude; they have been an important building material.

Gávdhos is the top of a great submarine ridge, which is tectonically active like Crete. Solution-notches in cliffs on the Cretan coast mark periods when the land was lower relative to the sea than it is now. The highest notch, up to 9 m above present sea level, marks an uplift of south-west Crete believed to have taken place in the sixth century AD. We noted a solution notch in aeolianites about 2 m above the modern sea level, which may correlate with this notch on the Cretan coast opposite. Remains of *Dendropoma*, coating some of these rocks at about the same elevation, are another indication of a higher sea level.

Vegetation

In previous centuries, travellers' accounts stress the treeless character of Gávdhos. An aerial view by the Venetian topographer Monanni in 1622 shows almost no trees except for a few patches of woodland in ravines and on the north-coast dunes. Captain T.A.B. Spratt (1851) remarked:

> the island presents to the eye a rather barren, unproductive appearance, having no trees or shrubs, excepting a few karoubs in the valleys, and a sort of stunted juniper growing amidst the blown sands upon the northern shore . . .

Even in 1952 Xan Fielding remarked on the barrenness of the island.

Gávdhos is far from barren today. More than half the island is woodland. Pinewoods (Pinus brutia) grow continuously over most of the hard limestone ridge, and in patches on the marls, especially in valleys, with a tendency to favour northern aspects. The biggest pines, about 60 cm in diameter, are no more than a century old, and the majority, forming woods, are 50 to 70 years old. Young pines are coming up everywhere. The pines threaten to burn at any moment.

The most remarkable trees are sea-juniper, *Juniperus macrocarpa*. Sea-junipers form big woods in sand-dunes at the mouths of the valleys on the north side of Gávdhos, and smaller stands on the marls. They are also scattered widely among other trees, not necessarily on sand, and occur as field trees among cultivated land; these isolated trees are bigger and older than those elsewhere, reaching nearly 10 m in height and 1 m in diameter and are 170 to 200 years old. This bizarre tree has a weird and gnarled habit; its boughs die back into bleached points of bare wood. The dieback of juniper was already characteristic by 1952, when it impressed Xan Fielding (1953):

> Half-buried in the blown sands . . . were the famous kedros trees, a species of stunted juniper, which looked like a regiment of corpses: some standing upright, like pagan prophets struck dead while uttering a blasphemy, each limb a pointed threat . . . But the rigor mortis of this sparse maritime forest was an illusion; these gesticulating, attitudinising trees were not only alive, but in fruit, bursting with brick-coloured berries.

6.2 Kastri, one of the principal settlements on Gávdhos, surrounded by encroaching woods of Pinus brutia, May 1989

Dieback seems not to be still continuing, nor is it all forty years old; probably there have been one or more episodes since Fielding's time.

Sea-junipers are the chief source of both timber and wood. The fruits, which are fleshy and taste like dried plums, are a speciality of the island and were once an article of export. They are still occasionally sent from the island for an unknown purpose. The third woodland tree of Gávdhos is *Juniperus phoenicea*.

As the human population has diminished, trees have increased. Sea-juniper was the first to expand, mainly on to former grazing land rather than terraces, in the mid-nineteenth century. Junipers, from the nature of their root systems, grew widely spaced, leaving gaps in which pines could later establish themselves. As they became more abundant, pines also became the first colonizers of terrace-land. In any one area, the pines are usually all of the same age. At present they are expanding much more rapidly than the junipers.

Some African plants occur on Gávdhos but not on Crete itself. For example, the desert undershrub *Periploca laevigata* is common on Gávdhos but does not reach Crete. The saltmarsh grass *Aeluropus lagopoides* just touches the southernmost tip of Europe.

Gávdhos, like the other satellite islands, is poor in the endemic plants peculiar to Crete. About one-tenth of the whole Cretan flora is endemic, but only four plants found on the islet have any claim to this status. One of these is *Silene greuteri*, a plant first discovered in 1982. Gávdhos has hardly any endemics of its own: we have occasionally seen the minute umbellifer *Bupleurum gaudianum*.

Certain of its phrygana and steppe communities also set Gávdhos apart from Crete. On the marls and metamorphics, a characteristic combination is *Globularia alypum*, *Anthyllis hermanniae*, *Cistus parviflorus*, *Thymus capitatus* and *Erica manipuliflora*, with frequent *Periploca*. This is a unique assemblage: we know of nowhere else where *Globularia* is a dominant undershrub. On hard limestone, there is a thin but definite steppe community in pockets of red earth, including for example *Ononis reclinata*, *Alium rubrovittatum*, *Linum strictum*, *Bupleurum glumaceum*, and a small form of the grass *Dactylis hispanica*. Other specialized plant communities include those of a spring-fed fen, a saltmarsh, sand-dunes and cliffs.

Animals

Little is known of the fauna of Gávdhos. It includes hares, partridges, and at least one species of snake. Terrapins are found in spring pools. The island has extensive, uninhabited, little-frequented coasts. We are told that the loggerhead sea turtle, *Caretta caretta*, nests on sandy beaches. Place names such as Phokóspilio, Seal Cave, indicate that the rare Mediterranean monk seal, *Monachus monachus*, frequents the island.

History, archaeology and land use

The island has been inhabited since the Neolithic, and for much of the time has been outstandingly and mysteriously prosperous. Bronze Age, Classical, Hellenistic and Roman antiquities litter the surface of the north-western part. The huge Classical to Byzantine site of Ag. Ioannis (Lávrakas), in the middle of the north coast, has been written about since the mid-nineteenth century. There are numerous walls, foundations and at least one quarry. From here Spratt retrieved a life-sized statue in Parian marble and presented it to the British Museum, where it still resides.

Medieval and later sea-charts mention 'Gozo' (often 'Gozo di Candia' to distinguish it from the Maltese Gozo) and 'Antigozo', but only as navigational points. The first useful map, Monanni's view of 1622, is full of place names that are still in use: for example, 'Camarelle', 'Alichie', 'Sarachinico', 'Potamo'. Several buildings are shown but not named, although the chapel of Ag. Ioannis can be recognized atop 'Capo S. Zuane'.

In the post-medieval period Gávdhos was visited by Muslim and Christian pirates, who tried to use it as a forward base. Monanni's visit was the result of one such raid. In the seventeenth century the island was sparsely and perhaps not continuously inhabited. According to Monanni its people came from Sphakiá, the part of Crete directly opposite. Pococke in 1745 reported that 'Gafda' was 'inhabited by about thirty families of the country of Sfachia . . . the Maltese corsairs supply themselves there.' It seems that the island went through a more populous period in the nineteenth century, perhaps as a refuge from troubles on the mainland. Spratt in 1851 reports '70 families, scattered over it in three or four hamlets and farms'. About 80 per cent of the island shows signs of once having been cultivated. Terraces, which cover much of the island, are well built and sometimes stylish, often of alternating great boulders and patches of small stones.

An unusual use for Gávdhos, from the 1920s to the 1950s, was as a place of punishment for political dissidents and sheep-stealers.

Gávdhos has a distinctive style of vernacular architecture related to the *kéntis* tradition of Crete. The typical house is a single room with a door in one of the long sides; windows are absent or much reduced. There is a triangular chimney in one corner. The main feature is a sea-juniper beam joining the middles of the end walls, in two unequal lengths held up by a huge sea-juniper post at the scarf-joint. Each length of the main beam is up to 6 m long and 35 cm square, about the size of the biggest juniper in the island today. Other buildings include a handful of grander houses of two storeys and others with ashlar blocks. Many of the houses and field-houses have been abandoned. There are two ruined windmills. At the west corner is a magnificent lighthouse, evidently designed by an architect of minarets. It was blown up in World War II and never reinstated.

Settlement patterns

Gávdhos has no village; the settlement pattern is of some twenty hamlets, of which half-a-dozen are still inhabited. These are connected by an elaborate network of footpaths and paved *kalderími* mule-tracks. It is surprising to find the hamlet tradition prevailing on a small island much in need of defence against pirates; most Aegean islands have the population concentrated in fortified towns. In 1622 the Venetians had plans to fortify the island, but these were never realized.

Much of the distinctive Gávdhiot way of life, its buildings, and its combination of agriculture and herding, are a survival of what used to be commonplace in Crete. Water is short. Springs are few and often precarious. Most of the hamlets, which are clustered around and on the hard limestone, are not near obvious water sources and appear to rely on cisterns.

Farming and herding

In 1990 actively cultivated areas had shrunk to about four per cent of Gávdhos. The main crops are grains (six-row barley, 'rivet wheat' *Triticum turgidum*, the old fashioned oats *Avena byzantina*, legumes, vetches, potatoes, artichokes, almonds, and figs. These, very unusually for Crete or anywhere in Europe, are still grown for local consumption. There is very little olive cultivation except for a recent plantation of irrigated olives between Sellí and Sarakíniko. Vines are rare.

Gávdhos, with cultivated land and recently-made roads, has weeds and other plants which go with human activities, but an odd and diminished selection of them. Thistles, for instance, are few but include the unexpected blue *Cardopatium corymbosum*; there is the unusual *Centaurea melitensis* instead of the expected *C. solstitialis* and we found no *Dasypyrum villosum*, *Scabiosa*, or *Dracunculus vulgaris*.

74

6.3 Old-fashioned cultivaton with cereals growing on terraces. Ambelos, Gávdhos, May 1989

Official statistics recorded 713 goats and 310 sheep in 1991. These numbers show an increase in flock sheep from the previous 10 years. In 1990 we were told that there were 1000 goats on the island, which agrees with our own observations. They are in the charge of two or three shepherds. There is a tradition of 5000 animals having browsed the island at one time. Browsing is now much less than the average intensity for Crete, but would have been very severe in the past, especially as the area available for browsing would have been much less than it is now.

Gávdhos is said to be good for beekeeping. The flowering season is short, but is supplemented by pines, which produce an exudation used as nectar.

Population

Censuses report a population of 471 in 1881. Since 1900 there has been a fluctuating decline, down to a minimum of 49 in 1981, followed by a rise to 119 in 1991. Although the decline is certainly real, the figures are official and should be treated with caution: they depend on how many inhabitants happened to be on the island when the census took place.

During the twentieth century, Gávdhiots have tended to lose their links with Sphakiá and to develop ties instead with Palaiókhora, capital of Sélinon, where many of them have houses in a Gávdhos quarter of the town and lands up-country. We were told that the Gávdhiots preferred to be part of Sélinon because 'it has lots of olives and we don't'.

There was still a school on the island in 1992 – with one pupil and one teacher. There is no resident priest, no doctor, and no mechanic.

Cultural uses and associations

In antiquity Gávdhos was called Claudias; the name is mentioned by various ancient authors, the most famous being the account of St Paul's last recorded voyage: 'And running under a certain island which is called Clauda, we had much work to come by the ship's boat' (*Acts of the Apostles*, 28, 16 c. 60 AD).

The *Stadiasmós* tells us that the island belonged to the city of Phoenix on the mainland of Sphakiá. Diodorus Siculus mentions a twin island called Kalypsos – evidently Gávdhopoula – and a temple of Aphrodite. This text has caused Gávdhos to be one of the many places identified with the Homeric island of Ogygia where the nymph Kalypso lived. Many visible Christian antiquities date from Roman and Early Byzantine times, when Gávdhos even had its own bishops. Many of the standing chapels today have been rebuilt on older foundations, and incorporate fragments of earlier buildings (Ay. Geórgios, Ay. Pávlos, Ay. Nikoláos).

Recreation and tourism

Several sandy coves on the north and east coasts afford landing-places but, until recently, there was no quay. Now there is a jetty, but it does not form a good harbour where ships can be safe from easterly weather. In summer there are sailings twice weekly from Palaiókhora to Gávdhos and back to Palaiókhora. In winter the service provided by the mail-boat is very irregular. Greek naval vessels call with stores from time to time. Military helicopters are called upon in emergencies.

Numbers of young people stay for variable times on Gávdhos, mainly in July and August, sleeping on the beach at Sarakíniko, and eating and drinking at the two small tavernas there. Two more tavernas are at the harbour of Karávi, where there are also a dozen or so very simple rent-rooms. In most of the hamlets there are coffee-houses with very meagre resources indeed. Spring in Gávdhos comes and goes very early. The pleasantest time to visit would be early in the year, but communications are then very unreliable.

Ecological dynamics

Gávdhos is the most eroding landscape in Crete, by badland formation, sheet and wind erosion. Where clays have been exposed, badland gullies have been forming, and in many places are still active. The gully system behind Pótamos in the north-west of the island is a dramatic example. It is already there on Monanni's view of Gávdhos in 1622. However, it adjoins a large archaeological site – primarily a pavement of sherds but with fragments of ancient walls incorporated into a terrace system built after the site was abandoned. The site has been greatly reduced by encroachment of the badland, which proves that the gully was not so extensive in Late Roman and Early Byzantine times.

Wind erosion is especially pronounced in these sandy landscapes. We were told that the island is often blasted by hot southern winds. We emphasize that erosion has little if anything to do with mismanagement of the land, but is an integral part of the Gávdhian environment. It is dependent both on tectonic uplift and on the nature of the rocks. Susceptible rocks do not occur so extensively in mainland Crete. Erosion has very little effect on agriculture (which has declined for other reasons) or on vegetation changes.

Gávdhos, as far as we know, has never been so wooded in historic times as it is now. Woodland has been increasing at more than one per cent of the island per year for several decades. and continues to do so. Increase of woodland, up to a point, adds to the diversity of habitat, especially for the commoner birds and other animals. However, the new woods destroy most of the distinctive plant life of non-woodland sites, without acquiring distinctive woodland plants. Few if any of the special plants of Gávdhos are adapted to shade.

Increase of woodland has almost certainly gone beyond the point at which it adds to the variety of habitat. But pinewoods have their own ecological dynamics involving fire. *Pinus brutia* is one of the most combustible plants in Greece. In the past ten years there have been numerous major pine fires in Crete, Kárpathos, and Rhodes, including one in the Soúyia area almost opposite Gávdhos. A big fire would be disastrous for the landscape and vegetation of the island. Pines would probably re-establish themselves afterwards, leading to a pine-and-fire cycle as can be seen on the island of Chíos. We emphasize that the cause is inherent in the nature of pine, and is not dependent on a particular source of ignition. Attempts to suppress fires would merely result in more fuel accumulating to cause a hotter, more catastrophic fire when it came. The stability of the Gávdhos landscape is not threatened by the extensive erosion, but is most seriously endangered by the increase of pine and by the prospect of a pine fire.

Landscape change

The unique landscape of Gávdhos and its unusual wildlife, archaeology and scenery is appreciated by visitors who are prepared to spend eight hours in an open boat getting to and from the island and by the inhabitants. The inaccessibility of Gávdhos has maintained the traditional ways of life disappearing rapidly on Crete and elsewhere. But whether this can continue in the face of national and socio-economic change is unclear. The inaccessibility of Gávdhos has encouraged depopulation and can make life difficult for those who remain: for example, the lack of a mechanic means that tractors and machines do not last. Most of the young people have left in search of a conventional lifestyle; those who are left are mostly elderly or aged.

Those who have chosen to stay on Gávdhos like the island much as it is. They are interested in preserving their island's character, though they would not object to a higher standard of living. Conditions are improving. Telephones have been improved; solar-electric cells provide modest amounts of electricity; roads have been made and small tractors imported; there is talk of a heliport. The present inhabitants would not, however, welcome uncontrolled development. They baulk at the thought of hoteliers building great resorts and tourists overrunning their island. The future of Gávdhos has been much discussed in the Greek press; outside developers have cast covetous eyes on it. So far they have been unsuccessful because land ownership is fragmented, and because it is difficult for visitors to be sure of getting away from the island in time to catch a plane from Crete. Currently the island is protected more by its relative inaccessibility, fragmented land ownership, and scarcity of water than by any specific conservation measures.

The future

The sustainable development of the island should aim to provide a setting in which local people will be willing and able to live simply but securely on Gávdhos; to reduce the fire hazard; and to make the island scene accessible to the outside world. We emphasize that these are modest objectives. They do not involve large capital works or opening the island to mass tourism. We envisage working with the islanders and not imposing someone else's strategy on them.

The general strategy of any future plans should, first, assist in providing facilities to allow interested visitors to study and appreciate the many special cultural and natural features of this island. Abandoned buildings might be restored to provide simple accommodation. Second, improved communications between the island and the mainland, especially in winter, are needed. This depends partly on improved telephone lines between Sélinon and the rest of Crete. Third, tourist development of the conventional kind, that would destroy local landscape and society, should be prevented.

Finally, measures are needed to reduce the dominance of pine and the fire hazard. This is a most necessary but most difficult task, and we cannot give a detailed specification of how it should be done. Pines are easily killed by cutting them down, but are likely to be more flammable dead than alive. Fire-breaks are probably ineffective unless very wide. If used, they should be contrived so as to incorporate existing fields and cleared land; they could be linked to a modest revival of agriculture. Any extensive work, especially if it involves bringing large numbers of people to the island, would itself be a fire hazard, and should therefore be done in winter or spring; this presupposes improved communications.

Since 1994 the development of Gávdhos has continued to be the subject of rumours in the press. The gravest proposal is a hare-brained scheme to build a large artificial port in the shallow sea around Gavdhópoula. The developers seem not to be deterred by the thought that this is a remote spot hundreds of kilometres from any markets or industries which the port might serve. The attempt, even if it fails, could hardly avoid having a devastating impact on Gávdhos as well as destroying Gavdhópoula.

Acknowledgements

This paper comes from our own researches, with the assistance of Anna Pyrgaki, in Gávdhos and in the Archivio di Stato and other archives in Venice.

The work was done with EEC funding as part of Contract: PL 890085 (EV4C-CT90-01, EV4C-CT90-0112), 'Threatened Mediterranean Landscapes: West Crete' between 1991 and 1993, from the Department of Geography, Cambridge University, in collaboration with Professor V. Papanastasis and his colleagues at the Laboratory of Range Science, Aristotelian University, Thessaloniki.

Chapter 7

Omalos Plain, Crete

I.P. Ispikoudis and V.P. Papanastasis

Introduction

High plateaux surrounded by peaks are a feature of the Cretan mountains. Omalos is the second largest of them, after Lasithi in the east, but it is the highest. It lies at the head of the vast Samaria gorge which falls from it to the sea on the south coast 16 km away (Fig. 7.1). The plain is 1045 to 1110 m in altitude and the steep slopes of the surrounding mountains of hard limestone reach heights ranging between 1120 and 1993 m. It is filled with hill erosion sediments of fine gravel and silt, fine sand, as well as dust blown from the Sahara to a depth of at least 10 m in places and with a thin, hard layer of bog iron ore. Much of the sediment is cemented. The gravel contains fragments of phyllite and quartzite. The losses of silt through swallow-holes are balanced by deposition of Saharan dust and inputs from erosion. The rivers of the Omalos drain into swallow-holes in the floor of the plain which are the most impressive of their kind in Crete.

Land use

The drainage of the Omalos has evidently changed as the swallow-holes have become more or less effective. Old Venetian maps show Omalos as a lake, the Lago di Omalo. There are seasonal wetlands today and a small permanent lake which is a valuable wetland habitat as well as a watering point for livestock. The area of the plain is about 800 ha. It is privately owned. The surrounding hills are state-owned with grazing rights held by the inhabitants of the neighbouring townships, Lakkoi and Epanochori. Agricultural land covers about 16 per cent, rangelands 32 per cent, forests 38 per cent and other land 14 per cent, including buildings, riverine vegetation, rocky land and a small pond. Important natural features which attract tourists include: the rock staircase (*xyloskalo*) which is the entrance to the Samaria Gorge; gravel fans which are a relic of Pleistocene glaciation and 180,000 years of age; and swallow-holes and caves. The Omalos plateau with its peculiar landforms, unusual plant and animal life, remarkable trees, characteristic buildings and field systems has a special place in Cretan history, legends and songs.

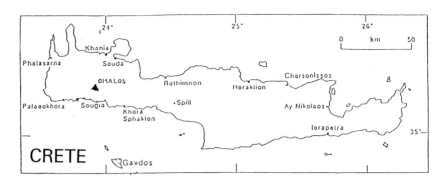

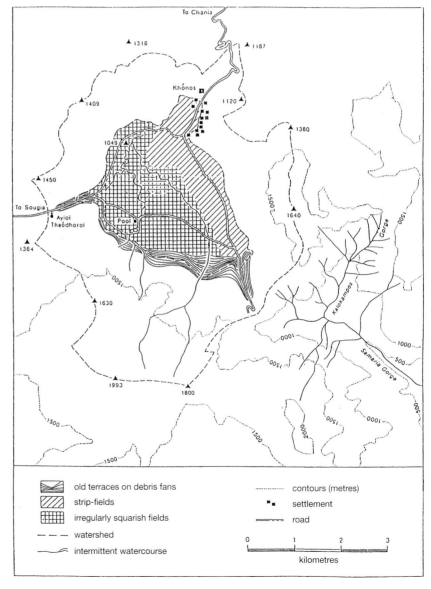

7.1 *Topographical map of the Omalos*

Flora and fauna

The rock limestone slopes are in places covered thinly and in others thickly with trees. Between the trees is phrygana and steppe vegetation. The silty floor of the plain, where not cultivated, has several distinct plant communities. Long uncultivated areas are covered by phrygana of various kinds. The main trees are *Cupressus sempervirens*, *Zelkova cretica* (an endemic), *Acer creticum*, *Quercus coccifera*, *Pyrus amygdaliformis*, *Crataegus heldreichii* and the rare *Sorbus graeca*. The phrygana is typified by *Genista acanthoclada*, *Anthyllis hermanniae*, *Euphorbia acanthothamnos*, *Erica manipuliflora* and *Berberis cretica*. There are many endemics which, in addition to *Zelkova*, include *Arum creticum*, *Sideritis cretica*, *Huetica cretica*, *Gagea amblyopetala*, *Cyclamen creticum*, *Chionodoxa cretica*, *Cerastium comatum*, *C. scaposum*, *Erysimum raulinii*, *Origanum microphyllum*, *Paeonia clusii*, *Phlomis lanata*, *Verbascum spinosum*, *Hypericum kelleri*, *Taraxacum* of the bithynicum group, *Tulipa bakeri* and *T. cretica*. Also, Omalos is the highest locality for the endemics *Petrormarula pinnata* and *Valeriana asarifolia*. Birds recorded include chukar partridge, woodlark, black-eared wheatear, stonechat, raven, chough, alpine chough, lammergeier, buzzard, and Bonnelli's eagle.

Settlement patterns

Omalos has its own regular and distinctive style of field-houses *mitata* for summer living, with a rectangular shape and walls of mud-mortared masonry 1 m thick. They have a flat roof of the *kéntis* type, with a great cypress beam (one measures 9.7 m long by 36 cm square, as big as any in the palace of Knossos). There are two churches, or chapels, Ay. Pandeleimon dated 1862 and Ay. Theodoros dating from the late-medieval period. Near the church of Ay. Pandeleimon there is the house and grave of Yannaris Hatzimichalis, a hero during the Cretan revolution of 1866–9 and President of the Cretan Government during the period of Cretan Independence.

In the past, the entire plain has been tilled, and cultivation has been extended on to terraces up the surrounding mountain sides. The main crops were cereals and fruit trees. This cultivation was combined with shepherding. Fields were cultivated every other year and cereal fields were grazed after harvesting. Most of the time, however, the plain was partially and inter-mittently cultivated, as is the case today, suggesting that there has always been a fluctuating agro-pastoral equilibrium. Two field systems exist on the plain: first, fields in narrow strips, often slightly terraced with many trees between them, and second, square fields with few, often older, trees between them. There has been little change in land use since 1945, perhaps a slight decrease in the agricultural land, with the cypress woodland becoming denser.

Socio-economic systems

Hunting and wild plant harvesting take place on the plain. For wild vegetables the area is renowned for the harvesting of stamnangathi (*Cichorium spinosum*), which is a great delicacy in Crete. Cropping is still taking place, but it is less important than livestock husbandry, which dominates. Forest stands are sparse and open and have no economic value. Only fuelwood is collected, mainly from the cypress trees which are very often illegally cut by the local people. There are no permanent inhabitants in the plain. The field-houses *mitata* are at the edge of the plain and they are divided between the two townships which have administrative jurisdiction in Omalos, Lakkoi and Epanochori (Lakkiotikos and Seliniotikos Gyros respectively). There are some new intrusive buildings (houses, hotels and restaurants) at the entrance of Omalos catering for the summer tourists visiting the famous Samaria Gorge. Schools also visit Omalos and Xyloscalo, the entrance of the Samaria Gorge. The Omalos Plain is the only place where students and the public can easily see the Cretan spiny-elm (*Zelkova cretica*) or the famous tulip, *Tulipa bakeri*. The two churches (chapels) are visited on their saints' commemoration days.

Literary and artistic associations

Omalos has a special place in Cretan history, legends and songs. It is well documented in the late Venetian period (1583) and there are numerous accounts of the Omalos Plain in the reports of Venetian governors. Omalos, being by nature inaccessible and easy to defend, was used by Cretan resistance fighters during the centuries of foreign rule as a refuge and a base for attack. The heroic exploits of the rebels gave rise to countless popular songs such as the well-loved *rizitico* (mountain village song):

> When will the cloudy sky be clear
> and come the month of February
> then I may take to hand my gun
> and don my belt of bullets
> and set off down to Omalos
> the path of the Mousouri. . . .

Tradition tells that on moonless nights one can hear the mournful lyre of a shepherd who was lost in the Tzani cave after the fairies had deprived him of his wits. Cretan lyre players claim that whoever learns the lyre from this shepherd plays the instrument to perfection and so they used to assemble here for master classes.

Significance and status of the landscape

The plain and its surroundings are rich in rare plants, with a high concentration of endemics, which is probably the third biggest concentration of endemics in Crete. There is the second largest population of *Zelkova cretica*, one of the world's rarest trees. The cliffs around the mouth of the Tzani cave have a unique combination of high- and low-altitude plants. This is the highest locality for the endemics *Petromarula pinnata* and *Valeriana asarifolia* and the lowest locality for the high mountain plants *Prunus prostrata* and *Aubrietia deltoidea*. Some of the cypresses, which are coppice stools, are at least 500 years old. Six big *Zelkovas* 2.1 m in diameter are probably of at least this age. Some of the pollarded tea-trees, 1.5 m in diameter, are the biggest in Crete. The lammergeier, Bonelli's eagle and chough are rare species throughout Europe and their Cretan populations are of global significance. The scenery of Omalos, with its surrounding high mountains, the Samaria Gorge, characteristic field systems, cultivation techniques, the field houses and the traditional pastoral activities, make it a most beautiful mountain plateau and it is one of the wonders of Crete.

The future of the area

There has been relatively little change since 1945, but the fact that the Omalos Plain has so far escaped modern agriculture does not mean that it will be unaffected in the future. Omalos is more fragile than most Cretan landscapes. Due to reduction of agriculture, cultivated land will decrease, while the reduction of pastoral activities will lead to more rangeland being taken by forests. Since 1945, cypress and pine forest cover has increased and it was denser in 1989 than it was in 1945. This may lead to diastrous wildfires. Since Omalos is en route to the Samaria Gorge, several new hotels, houses and restaurants have been built at the north-east edge which spoil the scenery. These buildings are likely to increase at the expense of the traditional field-houses, as more and more people visit Omalos to collect wild herbs or to go down the Samaria Gorge. There is a plan to construct a big reservoir on the Omalos Plain with a capacity of one million cubic metres, to collect water for irrigation. Intensive cultivation of the plain is a goal actively pursued by the local people and some governmental agencies. This is a potentially disastrous threat to the landscape.

The Forest Service and conservation groups are attempting to give Omalos full protection by including the Omalos Plain and its surroundings in the Samaria National Park. This is a dubiously desirable step since complete protection of Omalos from traditional human activities could destroy its unique landscape as surely as development.

The future objective for the area should be to maintain the traditional agro-pastoral equilibrium with moderate human intervention, so that people can visit it and enjoy its unique geomorphological, physical, biological and cultural values. This might be achieved by declaring it a protected landscape to become part of a Biosphere Reserve with the Samaria National Park as the core zone, Omalos being the manipulative or buffer zone and/or the stable cultural zone of the Reserve. This would mean that traditional human activities such as farming, livestock grazing, beekeeping, fuelwood collection and wild-herb (stamnangathi) collection would be allowed to continue without disrupting them with major changes. Government services need to be persuaded to accept such a strategy and local people given incentives in the form of subsidies to continue living and working in the area. European Union projects such as LEADER which favour agro-tourism should be exploited to help achieve these objectives.

Box 5

Balearic landscapes

M. Morey

Despite the extensive tourist development of their coastlines, the Spanish islands of Majorca, Minorca, Formentera and Ibiza retain some old and unusual farming landscapes inland. The plain east of Palma, the capital of the largest island, Majorca, still has some surviving cloth or metal-sailed windmills from the crowded forest of them which once pumped irrigation water to the forage-crop fields and cattle of smallholdings. The landscape was once dotted with farmhouses and small villages. Over-exploitation of the groundwater causing salinity, encroaching tourist development and the decline of an ageing population are leading to the abandonment of the farms and loss of the windmills in this former bay of the sea. The cereal cropping landscapes in the central plain of the island, characterized by similar one to two ha smallholdings, pine woodlands and small temporary streams, are also being abandoned by an ageing population, leading to scrub with more frequent erosion and fires. In the rocky, limestone mountains of the north-west of the island there are extensive terraced fields of crops and olives remarkable for their steepness and consequent high proportion of stone walls to field area. They are mainly parts of large (50 ha) landholdings (*possessio*) also used for hunting, but they are also subject to a decline in management, with walls crumbling and the fields eroding.

In Minorca large properties with farmhouses (*lloc*) and arid semi-natural pastures used to raise sheep and cattle are set in rolling terrain intersected by deep gullies and with scattered villages and pine, holm oak and olive woodlands. The area is important for Bronze Age monuments, endemic cushion plants which occur in the grasslands, and exceptional populations of birds of prey. The landscape originated from English domination in the eighteenth century and still resembles some English landscapes. The mixed stock and cereal farming landscapes of Formentera with characteristic small, stone-walled fields and the cropping landscapes of Ibiza with scattered country houses are also very rich in biodiversity and archaeological remains. As in Majorca, the maintenance of all these landscapes threatened by rural decline depends essentially upon the revitalization of farming through developing new products and new markets and support for the restoration of rural structures. Some encouraging farm tourism initiatives have begun as part of this process.

Box 6

Rio S. Lucia lowlands, Sardinia

G. Pungetti

The complex of reclaimed flat alluvial farmlands, brackish lagoons, marshlands and saltings in the delta of the Rio S. Lucia immediately south of Cagliari is in many ways typical of Mediterranean estuaries. Small, narrow parcels of cultivated land with greenhouse market gardening, vineyards, olives, almonds and carobs are bounded by hedges of prickly pears and trees with patches of eucalypt forest. Riparian and wetland vegetation with *Alnus glutinosa*, *Salix purpurea* and *Nerium oleander* and coastal macchia and garigue with *Juniperus phoenicea*, *Teucrium marum*, *Cistus* and *Asphodelus* form important habitats for resident and migrating waterfowl. There are salt works and industrial development in the lagoon and quarries along the river. The church of S. Lucia is the site of festivities, and the area is renowned for its coolness and used intensively for picnicking and informal recreation.

Industrialization, intensification of farming and manipulation of water levels after World War II led to pollution and salinization. More recently a decline in traditional farming with the abandonment of land and farmhouses, urbanization, road construction, increases in traffic, pumping of groundwater, illegal waste disposal and failure to restore abandoned quarry workings all threaten the integrity of the landscape. Overgrazing and uncontrolled fires and hunting have now been brought under control.

More integrated planning and management is needed if the great recreational, educational and ecological value of this landscape is to be better realized. The S. Gilla lagoon is protected as a Regional Natural Reserve and designated under the Ramsar Convention. National and regional forestry legislation also help to protect some features of the landscape. By improving the dialogue between the different departments involved in sectoral landscape and environmental issues, more vigorous and effective policies and programmes promoting sustainable development by a better balance between economic development and cultural and natural resource conservation might be achieved. A raising of general awareness and respect for the landscape through interpretation and education are important prerequisites.

Coltura Promiscua (mixed cropping)

Landscapes with mixed cropping (coltura mista or coltura promiscua) were normal until World War II all around the Mediterranean, especially in the lower mountain zones, and in some places they still are. Different cereals and vegetables were grown in rotations between olive trees, vines and fruit trees, frequently on large sequences of man-made terracettes. In the same zone multifunctional chestnut forests occurred, and at higher altitudes beech coppice for charcoal burning and high pastures for sheep grazing, as part of the transhumance system.

Many of the well-known Tuscan landscapes were based on this functional trinity of trees/grazing/arable land at different spatial levels: mixed cropping at the field level, mixed farming at the farm level and functional zonation at the landscape level. Amenity and the high biodiversity and historical value of these landscapes were unconscious by-products of well-organized farming and forestry at relatively low intensities for millennia. Landscapes were interwoven with local culture in all its aspects: nature, food, buildings, and oral history, art and language as well. The collapse of these land-use systems started locally at the end of the nineteenth century, accelerated rapidly after World War II and especially in recent decades due to intensification and specialization on one hand, and abandonment or extensification on the other.

Chapter 8

The Solano Basin, Italy

W. Vos

Introduction

Part of the larger Casentino Basin, the Solano is one of a series of inter-montane basins in the Tuscan Apennines of central Italy. The area of c. 10,700 ha is approximately located between 43° 40′ 00″ and 43° 47′ 00″ N and 11° 34′ 10″ and 11° 44′ 10″ E. It is confined by the water divisions of the hydrological basin of the 'Torrente' Solano, a tributary of the upper course of the Arno River. To the west the Pratomagno mountain range forms the interfluve with the Valdarno. Like many other cultivated landscapes of the Italian Apennines, the Solano Basin consists of an open basin with a clear altitudinal zonation. These zones range from Mediterranean to warm and cold sub-Mediterranean, up to mountain climate conditions. The strict Mediterranean climate zone is hardly met here. The warm and cold sub-Mediterranean zones coincide with the farming systems of the *coltura promiscua* or *coltura mista* (under c. 700 m), mostly on terracettes, and the grazed chestnut forest (*Castanea sativa*) (up to c. 1000 m), respectively. Both have been transformed or abandoned in recent decades. In the mountain zone beech (*Fagus sylvatica*) charcoal coppice (above c. 1000 m) and alpine pastures on high divides predominate. The former is changing towards high forest, while the latter are most often abandoned and subject to secondary succession. Formerly the sub-systems of this traditional landscape were functionally connected and the total arrangement was highly self-reliant (Fig. 8.1). Nowadays it is in part fragmented by intensification and segregation of functions on the one hand, and abandonment or extensification on the other.

Geology and geomorphology

The whole area is underlain by a thick base of sandstone-shale flysch sediments broken into blocks by faults with two dominant directions: northwest–southeast and northeast–southwest. From an ecological point of view some mineralogical and petrological differences are very relevant; the

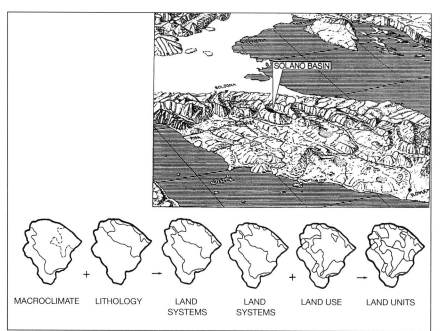

8.1 Location of the Solano Basin and sub-division into major landscape units. (Prepared with the help of Valentina Robiglio.)

MACROCLIMATE   LITHOLOGY   LAND SYSTEMS   LAND SYSTEMS   LAND USE   LAND UNITS

northern rocks have a larger proportion of silt and clay shales, a higher percentage of limestone and spary calcite as well as some dolomite. Locally this sandstone-shale base is covered by clayey sediments, which have a chaotic appearance and instability in common. They can be both calcareous and non-calcareous. In the valley bottoms, and on adjacent river terraces along the Solano River, alluvial sediments occur, in part covered by colluvium.

The lowest point of the drainage basin is at the Torrente Solano confluence with the Arno (345 m above sea level), and the highest point is on the Pratomagno (1537 m asl). The overall topography is dominated by a fine network of valleys and interfluves of a subdendritic river system, largely controlled by faults. Most valleys have an asymmetric form, gentle dip slopes facing north to east and steeper outcrop slopes lacing south to west. The former cover the largest area. This distinction between north-facing and south-facing slopes is strongly reflected in land-use and vegetation patterns. All slopes have been modified by various kinds of slope processes: flowing, heaving, slipping, falling and rolling, and washing off. Practically every slope is covered by slope deposits. Earthflows, slump and sliding are recent phenomena.

The upstream valleys are V-shaped; wider valley bottoms occur locally. Downstream, near the basin mouth, the Solano has formed an alluvial flat of a maximum width of *c.* 1 km, with some low terrace steps. In most cases the interfluves form sharp crests, only locally are they rounded to flat. The discharges in the basin are very rapid. The effects were demonstrated by the well-known flooding of Florence in 1966, to which the Solano Basin contributed.

Land-use history

Due to the rather isolated position of the Solano Basin, traceable influences of older cultures in the area are very scarce. Arezzo was, however, an important Etruscan centre, and therefore an Etruscan presence in the Casentino area from about 750 BC seems probable. In the first century BC this centre became a Roman municipality with numerous *coloniae* (farmlands) in the neighbourhood. Main roads crossed the Casentino area, linking Arezzo to the north and to the west. Remains of the Roman occupation have been found. Nevertheless, the whole area maintained the character of an un-exploited wild hinterland. During the feudal period the clergy acquired extensive properties all over the region. Benedictine monks gradually opened up the forest, but their activities were concentrated in the Camaldoli parts of the 'Foreste Casentinesi'. In the Solano Basin there are no indications of forestry practices in medieval times. From 1200 to 1359 the area was under the influence of city nobles, the counts Guidi of Florence. They founded various castles whose remains can still be seen. At that time the introduction of the *mezzadria* land tenure system took place: a sharecropping system based on self-sufficiency of the farmers and production of basic food for the land-owners in the city and also of some additional products. Mixed cropping was the normal practice. The land was worked from many isolated farms (*poderi*) around an administration centre (*fattoria*), the country house of the landowner. Commercial charcoal burning became important in the Casentino Basin in the first half of nineteenth century.

A dense population, that mainly lived from subsistence agriculture at the end of the nineteenth and the beginning of the twentieth century, created a landscape that was nearly completely in use by farmers and foresters. Four main traditional farming and forestry systems controlled the Solano Basin landscape. *Coltura promiscua* or *coltura mista* was a form of arable farming on fields where different crops were grown together, predominantly on small-holdings with mixed farming, including grazing as well as arable farming, horticulture, viticulture and some woodland. Chestnut forest management involved a multifunctional use of open chestnut groves with cycles of a maximum of 200 years. It included the exploitation of the forest for grazing, firewood, timber, poles, chestnuts for human and pig consumption, mushrooms, hunting, leaf manure and honey. Coppicing for charcoal burning focused on beech coppice with standards at higher altitudes, and other tree species in the lower *macchia*. Cycles of 15 to 20 years were normal. Charcoal kilns were made in the forests on small terracettes (*piazze*). Sheep grazing took place on high- and low-altitude pastures and fallow land; large flocks were moved every year to the coastal zone (*maremma*) for winter grazing (*transumanza*).

Population and settlement

Fluctuations in the population due to wars and pestilence have followed one another during the centuries. There was, however, a net population growth in the whole Casentino area till the second or third decade of the twentieth century. At the time of the highest population density, the traditional management systems of agriculture and forestry controlled the Solano Basin landscape entirely. Since the 1930s, but especially from the 1940s until the 1970s, the population decreased dramatically, mainly because of high emigration rates and, to a lesser extent, a decrease in natural growth. The population decline has been especially great at higher altitudes and in areas under *mezzadria* contracts. Nowadays the total population in the Solano Basin (which consists mainly of the municipalities of Castel San Niccolo and Montemignaio) is only about a third or a quarter of its peak. Moreover, the population is relatively concentrated in local centres, and is of a relatively high age. The rural exodus has resulted in a considerable reduction of areas under agriculture and forestry to about half of the peak exploitation reached in the 1920s to 1930s.

The present-day settlement pattern resembles roughly the historical one: large centres at the mouth of the valley, small centres in the middle of the agricultural area and both isolated farmhouses and clusters of farmhouses scattered over the agricultural area. Nowadays many of the latter are used as second homes for townspeople. The present-day land-use patterns also still reflect the traditional ones. Some characteristic features are that most holdings still practice mixed farming with grass, arable land, horticulture and woodland, *coltura mista* still occurring frequently. The grazing intensity of both cattle and sheep is low; mechanical power is the norm; chemical fertilization and crop protection are at a low level. Modern vineyards are limited to relatively small units. A transition has taken place from traditional forestry systems (coppices for charcoal, grazed chestnut groves) to both deciduous high forests for timber, short rotation coppices for fibres and extensive areas of coniferous forests for soil and water protection.

Flora and vegetation

Phytogeographically, the Solano Basin is located near the borders of two regions. The lower parts of the area belong to the Mediterranean Region, and the higher parts to the Central European Region. The vegetation of the Solano Basin reflects the transition of the Mediterranean-type climate to a mountain climate (Fig. 8.2). Forests cover the largest part of the basin, in which the typical sub-Mediterranean climax of *Quercus pubescens* and *Quercus cerris* preponderates. There are mixed oak forests on steep slopes and crests, mostly on calcareous materials, and chestnut stands on acid soils. *Carpinus* forests occur on cooler and wetter slopes, *Ostrya* forests on warmer and dryer slopes. Beech forests occur above 1000 m. Two different riparian associations occur with *Salix purpurea* and *Alnus/Fraxinus*, and often they are adjacent to each other and have many species in common. Their sites differ mainly in inundation frequency and soil development, the former being closer to the very dynamic riverbeds. On its lower side, the beech belt is adjacent to chestnut forests and mixed coppice of deciduous woodland. The upper limit forms a transition to a top belt of permanent pastures grazed by cattle and not fertilized. Grass species (*Nardus stricta*, *Avenella flexuosa*, *Festuca* spp.) and others dominate this vegetation. *Calluna vulgaris* and *Juniperus communis* form shrubland

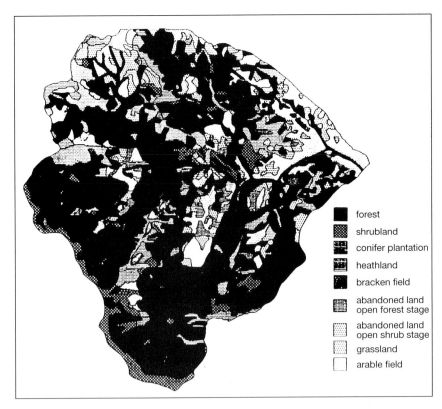

forest

shrubland

conifer plantation

heathland

bracken field

abandoned land open forest stage

abandoned land open shrub stage

grassland

arable field

8.2 Simplified vegetation map of the Solano Basin

locally. Because of their importance as a crop, stands of well-developed chestnut forest occur over large areas, mostly in the neighbourhood of small villages. Most chestnut forests have, however, been abandoned in past decades. Recent interventions are coppicing (frequently because of diseases) to transform them into production stands, or substitution by conifers. A natural modification of abandoned stands leads to mixed chestnut–oak forests.

Heathlands and related shrubland and forest communities are derived communities, replacing well-developed forests, and occur in or border upon the beech zone. Dense bracken stands frequently occur in the beech zone and in the upper chestnut zone. They may develop on sites that after cutting of the forest have been grazed for several years and then subsequently abandoned. *Pteridium* communities may naturally regenerate to forest, but closed bracken cover may obstruct this development for a long time. Several bracken fields have been planted with conifers. Grasslands with brome and fescue are common on steep slopes exposed to the south. Some consist of a semi-natural/natural *Spartium* shrubland community on steep rocky slopes with stony soils (*Xerobromion*); others are post-cultural, depending on recurrent human influences on deeper calcareous soils. Broom (*Cytisus scoparius*) forms several plant communities in combination with various other plant species, including: *Calluna vulgaris*, on steep and rocky slopes; *Lychnis flos-cuculi* and *Quercus pubescens* on abandoned terracettes and grasslands; and *Prunus spinosa* on rich, clayey soils. The communities on terracettes, previously in use as cereal fields, horticultural fields, or fields with sown grasses or Leguminosae, are characterized by an abundance of different plant species due to their pioneer phasing and the influence of previous land use. On deep-ploughed soils grasslands of *Molinia* and *Arrhenatherum* occur. Wet grasslands with plant communities of *Juncus inflexus* and *Mentha longifolia* occur in frequently inundated or waterlogged sites.

The value of the landscape

Landscape may be defined as a characteristic spatial arrangement of ecosystems, which confers a typical arrangement of visual space. The fact that the Solano Basin is just what one would expect such a traditional *coltura promiscua* landscape to be gives it its significance. It has no concentrations of endemic species, or of very rare plant and animal species, but it still has most of the characteristic spatial arrangements, and both forest and agro-ecosystems with the specific species of a typical *coltura promiscua* landscape in the Italian mountains. It is still a relatively well-preserved example of the historical and cultural heritage of the nineteenth century. In that sense, it exemplifies the sustainable integration of characteristic land-use practices with the natural physiography and ecological self-regulation dynamics. Given the low intensity of the land use, the extensive forests, and the location of the area on the extreme western wing of the Apennines, surrounded by well-developed forests (Vallombrosa, Foreste Casentinese), the upper Solano Basin may be very important for the development of the ecological infra-structure at the supra-regional level. Under these conditions the large predatory mammals that still occur in the neighbouring Central Apennine forests, including wolves and bears, may gradually migrate to or successfully be reintroduced in the Pratomagno forests.

To what extent the arrangement of ecosystems and their constituents are characteristic may be assessed by applying concepts from general information theory. The most informative parts of the landscape configuration may be identified by applying mutual information theory. Certain ecotopes have a higher mutual information value than other ones, that is they predict with a higher certainty their neighbouring ecotopes that together make the land-scape. This may be interpreted as a measure of their significance within the spatial configuration of a particular landscape unit. In another approach those ecotopes have been assessed that have the highest informative efficiency in a certain landscape. These ecotopes have the highest probability of indicating to which landscape they belong, and that they are the most exclusive for that particular landscape. This spatial information analysis at landscape level makes us conclude that within the Solano Basin the upper valley of the Solano river itself is the most informative (characteristic) part of the whole basin.

Threats

After World War II, land use changed radically in many areas like these, due to a dramatic change of socio-economic conditions. As a consequence the number of people active in agriculture and forestry sharply declined. There is no longer an economic base for the laborious traditional practices, and no market for certain traditional products such as charcoal, chestnuts and wool. On the other hand, where it may be profitable, subsistence agriculture has been replaced by market-oriented agriculture. Two main, directly opposite, trends prevail in these transformations. On the most suitable sites, where climate, land suitability and infrastructure make increased inputs profitable, intensification occurs, with market-orientation of produce, a high level of technology, efficient organization and layout (monocultures) and the introduction of exotic species. On the least suitable sites, where increased inputs are not profitable because of high altitude, or steep, rocky or isolated sites, extensification occurs with irregular management and abandonment of the land.

Even though the present-day landscape still strongly reflects the traditional land use, the culture which built it through the centuries is rapidly declining. The land-use system which developed from medieval times was oriented to self-sufficiency of food through a systematic, but balanced, use of the natural resources. In this region natural thresholds were not crossed, and continuity (sustainability) of production and environmental quality was achieved generation after generation. But, within a couple of decades, external socio-economic changes have made the low-input, multi-purpose agriculture and forestry lose its managing control over the landscape. And this process is still continuing. As a consequence, both the biodiversity at species and community level and the characteristic spatial arrangements of ecotopes, cultural elements and patterns are seriously threatened. The breakdown of the traditional land-use systems by extensification and intensification affects the landscape in different ways and at different levels (Table 8.1).

At the species and community level, biodiversity controlled by land use decreases. At the landscape level, the fine-grained arrangement of the traditional agricultural landscape is gradually replaced by a coarser, less characteristic pattern. The latter development also induces a decrease in biodiversity. Moreover, new elements such as coniferous plantations and monocultures of maize, sown grass or vines do not harmonize with the previous spatial arrangements but are widespread over the whole area without any landscape,

Table 8.1 Trends in landscape change

Land use transformation	Location	Processes	Possible landscape impacts
Abandonment	Old terracettes Other fields and pastures	Invasion of woody plants Secondary succession Run-off onto roads/paths Breakdown of stone walls	Risk of wild fires Vanishing cultural patterns Increased erodibility Increased slope instability
Intensification	Cultivated land Pastures Village-fringe	Monocultures Neotechnological measures (draining, irrigation, bulldozing etc.) Infrastructure/buildings	Decreased biodiversity Increased erodibility Air, water and soil pollution Increased traffic Noise/unrest Cultural disrupting patterns

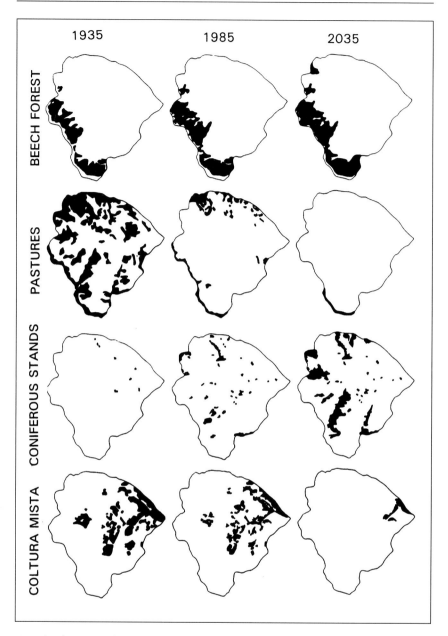

8.3 The decreasing landscape pattern diversity in the Solano Basin: 1935, 1985, 2035

ecological or cultural differentiation. Apart from this homogenizing process, the secondary succession on fields, grasslands and in forests also tends to erase the traditional spatial differentiation, in the end causing the same forest type to develop everywhere under the same climate and parent material conditions. Comparing landscape pattern maps for the years 1935, 1985, and a scenario simulation for 2035, reveals a striking and severe decrease in the pattern diversity of the Solano Basin landscape (Fig. 8.3). The present-day landscape shows the remnants of certain traditional Tuscan mountain landscapes. In another 50 years the patterns will have changed radically, and as a consequence, certain traditional Tuscan landscapes may vanish.

Even after decades of clearly negative trends, there are still no generally accepted strategies for the safeguarding of these landscapes, nor for a sustainable development of agriculture. Apart from some anti-erosion measures, stimulation of recreation and general urban planning principles, there is no integrated approach to planning and development of the cultural landscape of the Solano Basin. Nature conservation, as practised in the Foreste Casentinese in the Eastern mountain chain of the Casentino, is not applied to this ordinary, but characteristic Apennine landscape.

Box 7

Montado (Dehesa) of Portugal and Spain

T. Pinto-Correia and J. Mascarenhas

The pure or mixed cork, holm and mountain oak (*Quercus suber, Q. rotundifolia* and *Q. pyrenaica*) forests of the south-western Iberian peninsula in the region of Extremadura in Spain and Alentejo in Portugal have long been exploited for a variety of products. Cork for wine bottles is cut from the bark of the cork oak every nine years or so. The trees are pruned to harvest wood for charcoal manufacture. Pigs are fed in the autumn on the acorns to produce the delicious, expensive, smoked hams known as 'Jamon Serrano'. Sheep are grazed on the grass under the trees and, every few years, the fallow grass is ploughed to produce a crop of grain for a year or two.

This complex agro-silvo-pastoral system of land use has produced one of the most aesthetically pleasing and biologically rich landscapes in Europe. With the small oaks at densities from 20 to 80 per hectare the

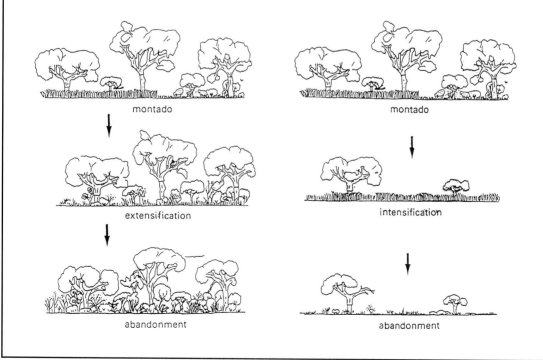

montado   montado

extensification   intensification

abandonment   abandonment

landscape is essentially open and savannah, or park-like, mostly rolling over fairly level or undulating terrain. The grasslands under the trees sparkle with wild flowers and the vast unbroken tracts of unintensively exploited and relatively undisturbed land provide habitat for a great variety of wildlife, notably rare and threatened birds such as the Spanish imperial eagle and black vulture.

Changes in farming now threaten the survival of these landscapes. Swine fever reduced pig raising in the 1960s. Cereal production has varied according to market conditions and the level of subsidies. In some places and at some times it has been intensified with the clearing of more tree cover; in others it has given way to more grazing or to natural recolonization by scrub. Cork production is beginning to be threatened by a change to plastic corks for wine bottles. The characteristic dehesa/montado landscapes depend upon a balance between all the different kinds of exploitation, but maintaining this balance is increasingly difficult.

The dehesa/montado landscapes are thus subject to both intensification to more productive monocultures of cereals or stock and to extensification or abandonment to scrub. In either case much of their cultural and ecological value is lost. Scrub encroachment may initially increase heterogeneity and biodiversity and new equilibria may be attained with more emphasis on grazing, forestry or hunting. Intensification through the CAP is more environmentally damaging, but is more localized and may be able to be ameliorated by agri-environment schemes. New forms of management based on new products and income sources are needed to maintain the multifunctionality of the montado.

References

Pinto-Correia, T. (1993) 'Threatened landscape in Alentejo, Portugal: the montado and other agro-silvo pastoral systems', *Landscape and Urban Planning* 24, 43–48.
Pinto-Correia, T. and Mascarenhas, J. (1999) 'Contribution to the extensification/ intensification debate: new trends in the Portuguese montado' *Landscape and Urban Planning* 46, 125–131.

Bocage (wooded farmland)

Before the clearances of Neolithic and earlier Mesolithic peoples, virtually all of Europe was afforested up to the limit of tree growth on mountains. On poorer soils and difficult terrain farming has never completely eliminated the tree cover, exploitation systems having evolved which integrate the use of the woods for timber and grazing with pastures, hayfields and some arable in the open clearings. The forest was pushed back steadily to produce more and more small fields, with the trees becoming confined to copses and field boundary hedges. These bocage landscapes, which are particularly characteristic of southern England and north-west France, retain much of the biodiversity of the forest in more open, woodpasture-like environments which are more congenial to most people. It is these Arcadian, multifunctional landscapes with high biodiversity and amenity which have come to epitomize our concept of the good life in the countryside and many are increasingly maintained by hobby farmers.

Chapter 9

The Weald of Kent and Sussex, England

E.A. Simmons

Introduction

The High Weald is an undulating, scarp and vale lowland landscape in south-east England. It was formed by an uplifting of the underlying rocks, the Wealden anticline, some 65 million years ago. Sandstones and clays are exposed in concentric bands resulting in rolling ridges and deeply incised valleys which are covered by a woodland mosaic, the remnant of a great oak forest which historically covered the area. The High Weald covers an area of 1450 km^2 and has a distinct topographic boundary as it is surrounded by the claylands of the low Weald which in turn are rimmed by the narrow ridge of chalk which forms the North and South Downs. The mean altitude is 73 m above sea level and the mean annual rainfall is 821 mm – slightly less than the mean for England of 836 mm. To the south the High Weald ends abruptly at the spectacular slumped sea cliffs whose gorse cover gives them the name of Fire Hills – from here the coast of France is often clearly visible.

Geology and geomorphology

The Romans knew the Weald as the Sylva Anderida or 'wildwoods' and the possibly related Saxon 'Andredsweald', or Andredswald, which once extended across south-east England, gives us the name Weald. The great oak forest that covered the area was the Saxons' 'Wald' and they were the first settlers to make substantial inroads into it. Their villages are still settlements today but the dominant field pattern dates from the later medieval period of the thirteenth and fourteenth centuries. The 'shaws' or thick belts of woodland which surround many fields are remnants of the ancient forest and the Weald is still one of the most densely wooded areas of England, with a tree cover of 11 per cent.

The origin of the Weald's diverse and seemingly topographically perverse drainage pattern – in which rivers break out to north and south – has been much debated, but the most recent explanation is founded on the idea of antecedent drainage, that is superimposed drainage from a cover of strata now destroyed (Whittow 1992). The basin of the Weald was covered by a chalk dome which first appeared in the early Tertiary. Rivers flowing further away from the central axis of the dome would have become large enough to keep pace with the repeated uplift of the Weald, so maintaining their north–south courses. The small north- and south-flowing rivers that ran down the flanks of the dome would ultimately have become closely adjusted to the east–west structures of the Central Weald, especially along the easily eroded clay belts. The three principal rivers of the High Weald, the Medway, Ouse and Rother, have created distinct landscapes where they form steep-sided clay valleys.

Denudation has removed the central dome of chalk, exposing older rocks beneath to form the High Weald. These rocks, known as the Hastings Beds, are some 426 m thick and comprise alternate layers of sand and clay. The geology of these layers is complex. The Wadhurst clay, for example, contains shales, shelly limestones, calcareous sandstones and ironstones, and occurs wherever river erosion has cut through the Tunbridge Wells Sands of the High Weald. Weathering of the sands has created cliff faces on valley sides, pierced by caves and widening into gills that form both chimneys and passageways. These forms are unique in south-east England and are thought to have been initiated by Pleistocene frost action. The sands of the Hastings Beds become hard, current-bedded sandstones which form the distinctive ridges of the High Weald. The ridges are relatively low but their scarps and adjacent vales, occurring concentrically within the Weald, create an impressive landscape with significant ecological interest. It has been said that 'nowhere in Europe is there a region of similar size allowing the study of such a variety of rocks and a corresponding variety of plant, animal and human life' (Brandon & Short 1990). The closest wooded landscape is the bocage of northern France.

Vegetation

The original forest cover is now highly fragmented by farmland, but substantial relict patches of it remain. Some of the farmland has escaped modern agricultural intensification, leaving examples of heathland, hay meadows and other semi-natural habitats. Woodland management is a key feature of landscape conservation in the Weald, where many of the woods are of ancient origin. The mixed deciduous woods are mainly of oak (*Quercus robur* and *Q. petraea*), beech (*Fagus sylvatica*), and ash (*Fraxinus excelsior*), with understories of hazel (*Corylus avellana*) and sweet chestnut (*Castanea sativa*). The steep-sided, wooded valleys or gills are important for pteridophytes, lichens, Atlantic bryophytes and water beetles. Their humid microclimate favours many species of more generally western distribution in Britain, such as the Tunbridge filmy fern (*Hymenophyllum tunbridgense*). The Tunbridge Wells sands support partly forested heathlands; Ashdown Forest, for example, contains some of the most extensive heathland habitat in south-east England, home to rare species such as the marsh genetian (*Gentiana pneumonanthe*), but is threatened by gorse and birch colonization in the absence of traditional grazing management. The High Weald meadows are of considerable importance, as many have not been subjected to agricultural 'improvement' but are still used in a traditional manner to provide summer hay and autumn and winter grazing and contain a very diverse flora including large populations of the green-winged orchid (*Orchis morio*). Several species from the above habitats have national biodiversity targets (Table 9.1).

The rural economy

Much of the Weald was initially cleared around temporary summer and autumn steadings used for grazing and pannage by villages on the surrounding higher and dryer chalk and sandstone ridges. Place names in the Weald are indicative of this. The suffix 'ly' or 'leigh' denotes a forest clearing, 'den' denotes a wooded vale and 'hurst' is a copse on a hill. Similarly some of the place names, for example Furnace Wood and Forge Hill, are reminders of the once flourishing iron-smelting industry which later played its part in shaping the landscape. The ironstone of the Wadhurst clay produced an ore which had a much higher iron content than other British ores, and the abundant forests supplied the charcoal needed for the smelting process. Coppice sustainability provided underwood to make charcoal to feed the furnaces, but timber felling for shipbuilding threatened the forest. An early conservation measure in the form of a statute passed in the reign of Henry VIII (1509–47) ordered that in every acre 'twelve standels or stores or oak' should be left. In the reign of Queen Elizabeth I (1558–1603), an Act forbade timber-felling to produce iron but there is evidence that the felling continued.

Water was the other requirement of the iron industry and this was provided by damming the steep-sided, narrow valleys of the forest ridges to create 'hammer ponds' to drive the water wheels. The power operated the large furnace bellows and the massive hammers to beat the iron ore. These hammer ponds are still in evidence today and are now havens for wildlife and quiet recreation. Other shallow ponds mark sites of ore extraction, for example, between East Grinstead, and Wadhurst where it is known the Celts mined iron ore – a practice that continued through the Roman occupation. The Saxons did not continue extracting ore and the iron industry fell into abeyance

Table 9.1 Species occurring in the High Weald for which there are national biodiversity targets

Species	Common name
Lepus europaeus	Brown hare
Boletus satanas	Devil's bolete
Muscardinus avellanarius	Dormouse
Triturus cristatus	Great crested newt
Argynnis adippe	High brown fritillary butterfly
Boloria euphrosyne	Pearl-bordered fritillary butterfly
Pipistrellus pipistrellus	Pipistrelle bat
Arvicola terrestris	Water vole

until it was revived in the mid-thirteenth century. During the sixteenth and seventeenth centuries the industry flourished, manufacturing cannon for export and home markets, but the last forge at Ashburnham closed in 1830 – outcompeted by the coke-smelted iron produced in the north of England during the Industrial Revolution.

Historically, inward investment in the Weald has come from those employed in the service industries, such as the medieval bankers and the merchants who invested in the rural industries of iron-smelting, tanning and weaving of the sixteenth and seventeenth centuries. In the 1500s the Weald was one of the wealthiest regions of England, but the Industrial Revolution of the late eighteenth and early nineteenth centuries saw the demise of all the local industries as coal and iron were found in abundance further north. This deindustrialization brought severe poverty, unemployment and social unrest, which found its voice in organized protests and direct action, including the breaking up of agricultural machines by protesters. Agriculture had become the mainstay of the rural economy and the protesters' fears that rural livelihoods would be lost following the introduction of new technologies finds an echo in today's Weald. A further wave of investment did flow in to the area during the nineteenth century through the process of gentrification. Improved turnpike roads from London led to an influx of wealthy newcomers who built some of the many mansions and parks which are now characteristic of the Wealden landscape, but one wonders about the extent to which this wealth trickled down into the local economy. This same question may be asked of the Wealden incomers of the twentieth century as the High Weald is still dependent on money earned elsewhere – no longer just from wealthy landowners but from the majority of the workforce who commute to jobs outside the area.

The Weald, with its access to the sparsely policed south coast, proved to be the ideal place for illicit smuggling operations. Centres such as Goudhurst and Hawkhurst flourished due to this trade in the 1740s. The death penalty for smuggling could also be invoked for poaching, which was seen as a crime against the ruling class, and there is no doubt that this sort of savage justice fuelled the class resentments so typical of the period. On a gentler note the famous children's books featuring Winnie the Pooh by A.A. Milne were set in Ashdown Forest, and many children still make the pilgrimage to Pooh Bridge to sail sticks.

Land use

A recent landscape assessment of the High Weald identified nine character areas which were defined not just in terms of their visual cohesiveness but also by the social identity of the area (Countryside Commission 1994) (Fig. 9.1). In most of these areas agriculture and woodland management, often on the same land holding, were the traditional use of the land. The small-scale topography has resulted in a small-scale agriculture, the traditional farm being a livestock holding owing to the moderate fertility and heaviness of the soils. The limits of the terrain for agriculture are evocatively drawn by Vita Sackville-West in her poem 'The Land':

But only a bold man ploughs the Weald for corn,
most are content with fruit or pasture,
knowing too well both drought and winter's heavy going.

The farmers of the Weald, bold or otherwise, have struggled against more than the physical limitations of the soil on which they farm. The very structure of the landscape rules out any large-scale enterprises and the historical and modern-day problems of Wealden agriculture are inextricably bound up with the scale and nature of this landscape.

Financial pressures on agriculture have forced many farmers out of business in the last 20 years. Recent census statistics from the Ministry of Agriculture (FRCA 1998) indicate that within the 71 civic parishes in the High Weald AONB the total agricultural area fell by nine per cent from 1986 to 1996. The High Weald is predominantly livestock country with pasture rotated on a holding as a ley. The traditional bias towards cattle and sheep remains: of the 105,000 ha in agricultural land use there are 59,000 ha of permanent pasture and 28,000 ha of crops (Countryside Commission 1994). This is not surprising as 57 per cent of the land is of only moderate productivity, classed as Grade 3, with less than three per cent Grade 1 or 2, or highly productive land. From 1986 to 1996 permanent grassland declined by 7.5 per cent and crops and fallow by 19.4 per cent, replaced in part by the increase of 9.4 per cent in rough grazing. Farm woodland increased very slightly (1.4 per cent) to give total farm woodland cover of 11 per cent. Horticultural crops have declined and oilseed rape and, latterly, linseed increased. The loss of orchards and hops, where they occurred on the better land in the eastern end of the High Weald, is significant for the landscape.

Making a living from farming in the High Weald has become more difficult as livestock prices have plummeted and the arable sector has not been able to compensate. A new breed of farmer has taken up the challenge in the High Weald: the 'hobby' farmer who supports the holding by income from outside agriculture. It is estimated that these people make up some 20 per cent of farmers. What is significant for landscape conservation is the fact that they often embark on a farming enterprise with no previous experience in either agriculture or countryside management. Sixty-five percent of farms in the High

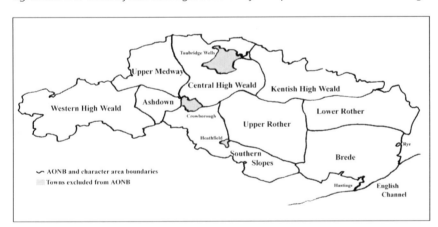

9.1 The nine character areas defined by the Countryside Commission's landscape assessment of the High Weald

Weald are now part-time enterprises. In 1982 there were 1027 full-time farms but by 1992 this had fallen to 870.

The Forestry Commission manages some of the woodland for timber and recreation, but much of the ecologically significant woodland is in private ownership. A feature of these woodlands is often a lack of management; either because their small size renders them uneconomic or, alternatively, because the landowner lacks the resources or the expertise to undertake management. An initiative, 'High Weald Design', set up to produce furniture from local timber has been successful in raising awareness of the Weald's woodland resource. Although the coppice industry has suffered decline in recent years, a burgeoning market for hazel coppice to make garden products has led to a revival of this practice. There is a regional partnership, Weald WoodNet, partly funded by a European Life project, which encourages the long-term, sustainable management of woodlands, both in the High Weald and in the surrounding area. By linking producers and buyers it aims to increase the use of local timber and develop new markets for it. Another local wooden product is cricket bats. The village of Robertsbridge is home to the company Nicolls which makes cricket bats from willow grown in the wet pastures of the Rother Valley.

Historical monuments

Notable architectural features of the High Weald include the restored windmills which stand on the sandstone hillocks or 'hyrsts'. Timber-framed houses – some dated earlier than 1500 – are still to be found, and wooden weatherboarding is characteristic of some Wealden houses. Wooden church roof tiles are also found, although the red local tiles are more common on frontages and roofs. Sandstone was used rarely, being reserved for buildings of local importance, such as the church in Goudhurst or the house of the author Rudyard Kipling at Batemans in Burwash. From 1902 to 1936 Kipling lived in a sandstone house built for an ironmaster in 1604. The Wealden landscape was the inspiration for many of his Sussex stories and poems. The two main towns of the Weald, Cranbrook to the north and Battle to the south, are very different. Battle commemorates the Battle of Hastings in 1066 when William of Normandy defeated the Saxon King Harold, changing the history of England for ever. Cranbrook has traditional white weatherboarded houses and is close to the fruit-growing area of the Kentish Weald. In the mid-nineteenth century it was home to a colony of artists centred on the painter F.D. Hardy. Nearby, the famous garden at Sissinghurst Castle, created by Vita Sackville-West and Sir Harold Nicolson, surrounds an Elizabethan house and is one of the best loved, most visited gardens in England, attracting 350,000 visitors per year.

Landscape change

The High Weald economy consists of very small firms. Agriculture and tourism are the two largest overall employers, but agriculture, forestry and fishing account for only five per cent of the total working population. The majority of the population is engaged in the service industries. At least 70 per cent commute to work outside the area, which means the villages turn into commuter or retirement settlements. As a result house prices soar and young people leave. A lack of transport and other village services increases pressures on local communities; a 1992 survey showed 75 per cent of rural parishes have lost their daily bus services, 39 per cent have no shop and 51 per cent no school.

Currently the use of land for forestry or agriculture is outside the planning system, as it is not classed as development. Changes in the agricultural landscape from the selling up and subsequent fragmentation of holdings poses a real threat to the landscape. Direct impacts of agriculture, including the lowering of the water table and the leaching of fertilizers or pesticides can have local impacts, for example in the river valley landscape areas. Throughout the High Weald traditional landscape features such as hedgerows and ponds are frequently neglected; this is sometimes due to the loss of traditional countryside management skills when farmers sell up to newcomers, but is often also a result of the declining agricultural workforce. These individual landscape features impart structure and cohesion to the landscape and the incremental changes due to lack of management can have far-reaching impacts over time.

Traffic management is also a serious problem, which is exacerbated by the large numbers of residents commuting to work. Tourism may generate some much-needed income for the High Weald but will only be compatible with the landscape if the low-volume/high-spend sector is actively encouraged. The undulating nature of the topography is such that the landscape can absorb significant visitor numbers, although the sunken lanes and rural roads may not be able to sustain traffic much above present levels. Urban areas make up some 4 per cent of the area and non-agricultural land 24 per cent, but there are pressures for further development adjacent to the High Weald. In the Low Weald near Horsham there are plans for some 58,000 new houses. Urban-edge development already poses a significant threat in the western High Weald as facilities such as garden centres, golf courses and superstores expand in number to meet people's needs. Vernacular buildings often experience a change of use, which may result in unsympathetic alterations that change their character. The interest in equestrian pursuits ('horsiculture') in the High Weald, although keeping land grazed, often results in a subdivision of fields into pony paddocks with poor, weedy grass swards.

Overall, pressure on the Weald may be aggravated by the lack of a decision-making body in the Weald itself. None of the major county towns falls within the Weald (Brandon & Short 1990) and so the perceptions of those making key decisions about its future are those of the outsider.

Protection and management

In Britain the concept of 'Protected Areas' was slow to be enshrined in law, and when the *National Parks and Access to the Countryside Act* was passed in 1949, the rate of designation of protected areas was similarly slow. Prior to the 1949 Act the Forest Ridges of the High Weald had been suggested for designation and in 1968 the proposed area was enlarged to include the whole area of the Hastings Beds (Anderson 1980), but it was not until 1983 that the High Weald was actually designated as an Area of Outstanding Natural Beauty (AONB), the fourth largest of the 40 such areas now designated throughout England and Wales. The primary purpose of AONB designation is to conserve and enhance natural beauty by tightening planning control. The recognition is international, falling under Category V Protected Landscapes classified by IUCN (the World Conservation Union).

The High Weald AONB is included in the slightly larger High Weald 'Natural Area'. The Natural Areas of England are not designated areas but rather areas with a common ecology that may be best conserved by a co-ordinated approach. They are part of English Nature's framework approach to achieving nature conservation objectives throughout the English landscape. Each Natural Area has a written profile of its nature conservation interest which highlights key habitats, species and features of geological importance and proposes objectives to conserve them (English Nature 1997).

In the High Weald there is a comprehensive committee structure in place which aims to address issues threatening the integrity of the area. The High Weald Forum is a partnership of 13 local authorities and 19 organizations representing the main land husbandries of agriculture and forestry, together with recreation amenity, water and conservation interests. In 1995 it produced a substantial management plan intended to be of wide use both as a strategic planning tool and as a basis for more localized management planning. The High Weald Management Plan (The High Weald Forum 1995) is complementary to statutory planning policies and guidance and proposes specific actions to conserve landscape character and foster a viable countryside. It identifies key topics including landscape, cultural heritage, nature conservation and built development and presents general management aims and policies in respect of these. It takes these proposals one step further towards implementation by making recommendations from the Forum as a whole to be achieved as actions by key partners.

An exciting new Land Management Initiative (LMI) funded by the Countryside Agency (the statutory body in England for landscape protection) and the Environment Agency is attempting to address just such issues via a programme of research and the development of a new agri-environment scheme specifically for the High Weald. A pilot area in the centre of the AONB will be the focus of the new scheme which will adopt an integrated land management approach, conserving and enhancing landscape, biodiversity and cultural heritage by supporting the viability of farming, woodland management and the rural economy (Land Use Consultants 1998).

In addition, Countryside Management Projects (also part-funded initially by the Countryside Agency) are active within the region. The Kent High Weald Project directly involves itself in heathland and orchard restoration, wildflower meadow conservation projects and hedgerow, woodland and parkland tree planting and management. It works with local people who contribute over 1000 volunteer work-days per year to enhance the landscape and improve access opportunities. It also administers a local Countryside Grant scheme which enables landowners to obtain a substantial proportion of the cost of undertaking conservation work. This has been particularly successful in promoting pond restoration.

Conclusion

The rate of decline of this significant landscape is increasing. It is encouraging that the different interest groups which concern themselves with the conservation of the High Weald are all converging towards the same conclusion. That is, that, in common with many traditional landscapes, the economic difficulties of small-scale farming dominate the past and present High Weald, and unless these are addressed the landscape and its valuable ecology and cultural heritage will continue to have an uncertain future.

Box 8

Tasman Peninsula, Tasmania

J. Russell

Spectacularly dissected coastal scenery with deep bays, cliffs up to 280 m high, offshore stacks, arches, blowholes and platforms surrounds the hilly mixed-farming landscape of the Tasman Peninsula. Wet and dry sclerophyllous eucalypt forests and woodlands and coastal heaths are interspersed with pastoral and agricultural clearings in the floors of the valleys between the sandstone and dolerite hills rising to 500 m summits. Some of the short streams in the valleys are seasonally intermittent. The first substantial European settlement took place from 1830 with the establishment of convict stations. The land was cleared for agricultural subsistence and the forests logged for both local use and the export of timber. After the closure of the penal system in 1877 extensive development of apple and pear orchards and dairy farming took place, based in scattered small farm holdings, to supply the European market. Small towns grew up, mostly at old penal sites. About half the land is held privately, the remainder is state-owned.

Aboriginal middens and the remains of the nineteenth century penal sites, many in ruins, are of great archaeological importance in the history of the early foundations of the modern Australian nation associated with convict transportation from England. The area is also of importance as a recreational resource and its beautiful scenery has attracted spreading coastal holiday-home development. The main farm enterprises of orchard fruit production and dairy farming both collapsed after World War II, and the rural economy is now more diverse with poultry production and forestry after the planting of Monterey pine (*Pinus radiata*) on old dairy farmland. Hobby farming has helped to maintain some farms and is spreading. Tourism has become a mainstay of the economy, but the economy and the landscape remain vulnerable and dependent on sympathetic development. The entire peninsula is on the Australian National Heritage Commission Register of the National Estate, listed for both its historical and natural features and several areas are designated as Historic Sites and National Parks under the Tasmanian *National Parks and Wildlife Act* 1970.

Box 9

Banska Stiavnica, Slovak Republic

L. Miklos

Mining for precious metals has moulded the landscape around Banska Stiavnica since Celtic times. The natural hornbeam (*Carpinus betulus*) and beech (*Fagus sylvatica*) forests of the mountains and valleys of this part of the Carpathians have been cleared and replanted several times to provide timber and fuel for the metal industry and mixed farming, producing a very diverse pattern of fields, meadows, pastures, forests, lakes and reservoirs set amongst impressive rock formations. Dispersed settlements are linked by winding roads. Tourism and hunting help supplement the deeply depressed local economy, now based on livestock farming following the working out and closure of the mines.

Abandonment of the mines, fields and houses, leading to natural succession back to forest and siltation of the reservoirs, now threatens the character of the landscape, which is based on the diversity and harmony of man-made features. Many reservoirs have disappeared; only some 30 of an original 60 still survive. Plantation forestry with spruce (*Picea abies*) has been extensive. Transport of materials in and out of the area is difficult and expensive. The population is falling and gypsies have settled in some abandoned properties.

The economy of the area and the maintenance of the cultural landscape which stems from it is seen to depend upon the success of local governments in attracting new industrial and other economic activities. Development plans place heavy emphasis on new industries, but others believe that the future of the region lies in its natural, historical and cultural resources and on agro-tourism and eco-tourism based on them. The town of Banska Stiavnica contains many historical monuments and is listed under the UNESCO World Cultural Heritage Convention. The whole region is designated a Protected Landscape Area and many other local attractions, including the oldest and best known arboretum in Slovakia, constitute a tourist resource with the potential to revitalize the town and its surrounding landscape.

Part Three
Landscape conservation

Chapter 10
Identifying threatened, valued landscapes

D. Bruns and B. H. Green

Introduction

All land cannot be given the same priority for protection, or for planning and management. Even with the modern, powerful, all-pervasive approach to environmental management of sustainability in land and resource use, some focus of effort or activity and thus some selection of territory is inevitable. Some parts of landscapes may need to be more intensively exploited in order to protect others. The selection of nature reserves and of other areas of special wildlife interest, would be difficult to envisage in the absence of an accepted hierarchical classification of species and biotopes. Despite their essentially abstract nature, such classifications are particularly useful and can also be practical tools for the selection of special landscapes. Once recorded, described and classified, landscapes and landscape types are amenable to evaluation in a similar way to that used for species and biotopes. Thus threatened and valuable landscapes may be identified from the basis of systematic inventories of all regional or national landscapes (Chapter 3).

Survey

The classification and evaluation of landscapes nonetheless presents some conceptual and practical problems. Reluctance to accept landscapes as geographical or natural units which can be described, classified and valued is often related to three difficulties:

* whether landscape units with a clear identity can be recognized;
* whether such units are unique or repeatable; and
* on what scales landscapes should be defined and evaluated.

These issues are linked. Expanding from the well-known idea that traditional geographic descriptions are first based on topography and geology, the grouping of geographically defined areas into similar kinds is a logical next step. If one adopts generalized large-scale territorial units such as mountains, estuaries, valleys, escarpments or plateaux, then the very existence of these words testifies to their acceptance as genera of pertinent landscape types (Troll 1950). European landscapes have been broadly classified (Schmithüsen 1963, Neef 1967), most recently into thirty main types, combining climate and vegetation with scenery (Meeus *et al.* 1990) (Table 3.1). Smaller landscape units are derived by subdividing larger ones. By introducing land use into landscape classification, units of great practical utility at smaller scales may be defined (Blankson & Green 1991). Quantitative methodology, including multivariate statistical analysis, may be used to classify recorded geographical attributes from maps in much the same way as plant records from quadrat samples are grouped into associations (Chapter 3).

To ensure representative samples, and for the purposes of quantitative analysis and systematic landscape evaluation, inventories need to be complete. For example, the Swiss fen and bogland inventory includes all land which is geographically classified as fens and bogs, and on this basis identifies units of national importance (EDI & BUWAL 1991). In German biotope mapping projects entire states are scanned for features specified in survey manuals (Jedicke 1994). Sampling great numbers of landscape qualities facilitates extensive search runs. Thus the geographic distributions of certain types of bog or hedge may be mapped, associated species of fauna and flora located, and indications of ecological dynamics and landscape change obtained. The presence of particular features, or specific groups of features, which define landscape character (Table 10.1) may help to identify individual landscapes as typical, authentic, complete or diverse. Thus, statistically sound evaluations of landscape are conceivable. In a landscape monograph on European landscapes, Gulinck and Múgica (1997) made three assumptions on which value categories were proposed:

- value categories can be recognized;
- landscape valuation is possible; and
- all landscapes have a value which is an integration of perceptual, ecological, and sustainable functions.

To facilitate research into landscape trends, particularly to attempt prognoses of landscape futures, and to substantiate landscape threats, inventories need to be repeated at intervals, and multi-temporal analysis carried out (see Chapter 8). So in summary the results of complete landscape surveys include:

- a widely accepted typology of landscapes;
- systematic inventories of landscape features; and
- regular repetitions of inventories to monitor change.

Evaluation

The concept of 'threatened, valued landscapes' is based on an approach which uses both objective and value judgements at different stages of the decision-

Table 10.1 Widely applied landscape descriptors deriving from national and international approaches

Functions	Landscape areas	Landscape elements	Direct human interests

Social
(perception + culture)
	Openness versus
	  closedness[1]
	Spatial patterns (field size,
	  distribution, diversity)
	Boundaries (water/land,
	  land cover types)
	Naturalness[2]
	Habitat type of preference
		Geological formations
		Settlements and cultural
		  monuments
		Linear features (hedges,
		  walls, fences, rivers,
		  forest edges)
		Punctual features (trees,
		  ponds, monuments)
		Archaeological sites
			Scenic outlooks
			Scenic roads
			Tranquillity
			Access to the landscape
			Coherence
			Accessibility
			Cultural identity
			Safety

Environmental (ecological)	Water retention functions Water quality Habitat diversity Protected areas	Key species Protected species Linear and punctual features[3]	Eco-tourism Educational facilities Human health

Economic
(sustainable)
	Land-use intensity
	Crop diversity
	Degree of abandonment
	Rate of urbanization
	Adequate soil/land use
	Traditional management
	Organic farming
	Population density
		Prevention of soil erosion
		Domestic species/
		  genetic diversity
		Degree of fragmentation
		Linear and punctual
		  features[3]
			Tourism/ recreation
			Regional products

1 Openness versus closedness refers to the degree of forest cover or structural density created by (higher) linear and punctual elements.
2 'Naturalness' refers to how close the actual vegetation is towards the potential natural vegetation, e.g. how much the actual land use reflects the natural climatic and soil conditions, or how many remnants of the original natural vegetation are left.
3 Linear and punctual elements can play a role for all three functions.

Source: Waschem *et al.* 1998

making process. It attempts to provide answers to two main questions. First, is there a threat, or the likelihood that a landscape will be threatened? Second, is the landscape worth conserving, and why? Answers to the first question lead to the identification of landscapes in need of investigation. Answers to the second question lead to the less obvious process of landscape evaluation to determine those landscapes which are most cherished and where, therefore, any threat causes much greater concern. The sum of the two processes is selection.

The identification of those landscapes which are threatened is usually far easier to determine than whether a landscape is worthy of conservation. Threats through, for example, changes such as those brought about by modern agriculture involving great loss of features such as hedgerows, or lowering of water tables by drainage, can be objectively measured, as can more subtle changes in the fine grain of landscapes such as their biodiversity. Monitoring of key features or species can provide a very sensitive indication and early warning of change. Such studies are perhaps best developed with farmland birds (Campbell & Cooke 1997), but other integrating indicators, such as field size, have also been used and elaborated into a sophisticated monitoring sampling system (Bunce *et al.* 1993).

Attempting to decide which threatened landscapes are most deserving of conservation is a more difficult, subjective process. The existence of threat, or actual change, is, in itself, something which adds to value, for surveys show that people often seem to prefer existing landscapes rather than anything they might change to. O'Riordan *et al.* (1993) showed visitors paintings of a variety of different landscapes which might develop in the Yorkshire Dales National Park in Britain under alternative policy scenarios. Most prefered the status quo even though some of the alternatives were arguably more visually attractive and clearly likely to be richer in biodiversity. Hunzinger (1995) arrived at similar results in perception studies of abandoned Swiss alpine scenes. Since most European landscapes like these are cultural, and it is impossible to freeze social and economic activity within them into a time warp, conserving them resolves essentially into a process of attempting to identify and then protecting those features generally regarded as making an essential contribution to their character.

Landscape surveys attempt to reveal this information about the area, age, amount or number of features, structural diversity and other landscape properties. This information is amenable to many kinds of quantitative measurement. At the most rapid and elementary level, numbers of landscape features, for example trees, may be simply classed as, few, several or many. To convert such measures into value, these classes can be ranked for ordination, or rated, if ratios between classes can be fixed. In ordinal ranking, few/several/many could, for example, be translated directly into low/medium/high value. In rating, if a 'few' trees were measured as one to five per hectare, and 'many' as 10 to 30 trees, cardinal numerical values may conceivably be attached to the evaluation as well by aggregating the measures for different landscape features. In practice ordinal rankings are most commonly used in conservation since, because of the different quality of landscape properties included in surveys, one cannot numerically compare like with unlike for there are no common parameters.

Landscape appreciation

The difficulty lies in converting this information into measures of value. In the assessment of landscape the category 'many' from 'few/several/many' or 'large' from 'small/medium/large' does not necessarily equate with increased value. 'Beauty lies in the eyes of the beholder.' If a travel brochure advertises 'The Northern Coast – A Landscape of Towering Cliffs' grandiosity is automatically converted into tourism value. People who enjoy seemingly endless vistas of tall cliffs might agree. Other people might prefer a countryside where small is beautiful. While the scale and measurement might be the same in both cases, the evaluation results are not.

People undoubtedly enjoy particular kinds of landscape. But precisely what properties of landscape give them pleasure and why they do so is more difficult to define. Early observers at the time of the Romantic Movement of the late eighteenth century followed Gilpin in their interest in the aesthetics and enjoyment of 'picturesque' scenery, distinguishing between the 'sublime' consisting of majestic views, usually of mountains, coasts or rivers with cliffs, chasms and waterfalls, which instilled fear, and the gentler 'beautiful' of the more familiar farmed countryside. The literature on the aesthetics of landscape tends towards atavistic explanations of landscape preferences in which landscape characteristics that in the past conferred survival benefits to the species are still favoured aesthetically. Appleton (1975) identified 'prospect, refuge and hazard' as three key human survival properties of landscapes and argued convincingly for their preference in landscapes today. Thus human evolution in savannah landscapes is said to be why people like the small-scale mixture of trees and fields in old European farmed landscapes. The same wood pasture pattern is also reflected in the traditional design of parks.

Subtle landscape characteristics such as 'coherence', 'cultural identity', 'accessibility', and 'safety' or 'security', which are difficult to define, let alone measure, are thus important in landscape evaluation. As in other value systems, whether for postage stamps or silver spoons, 'rarity' and 'diversity' are also important elements which determine the value of landscapes and landscape features. Two or three centuries ago, wild landscapes were common and to most were places of fear and dread; now that they are much rarer, they are widely revered. This example also serves to demonstrate that landscape preferences cannot be totally atavistic, fixed in time; on the contrary, appreciation can change as the landscape itself changes.

Diversity is a key element in ecological evaluations, but, despite the global trend towards species and landscape uniformity, high diversity is not automatically of high value (Plachter 1995). First, one needs to establish whether the goal is genetic diversity, species diversity, habitat diversity, or regional landscape diversity. Second, references must be given, both in space and time. Forests commonly, in most regions, have the highest biodiversity of all existing habitats. Grasslands and hedges and other habitats have lower biodiversity, and if maximum biodiversity were the paramount management objective, would have to be converted into forests. But grasslands contain many species not found in forests which would then be lost. Clearly the frame of reference is crucial; in this case a mixture of habitats would be necessary to maximize regional diversity. In landscape conservation it is usually the specific landscape character which is of interest, and the spatial reference would be the matrix, or mosaic, of the lie of the land. Diversities of landscapes of similar type may thus be compared with each other. For evaluation it would be necessary to establish the optimal diversity of the specific landscape type. In multi-temporal analysis, the diversity of the present matrix might be compared to those of the past, or those of a future scenario.

In modern conservation preserving the 'typical' (not to be mistaken for the average) and maintaining the natural and historically derived forms of land use in 'authentic' and unimpaired conditions are also becoming important goals. Table 10.2 includes some goals and criteria identified from the literature,

123

which have been employed to establish the 'worth' of a landscape. Measures are presented with which to apply each criterion in practice.

Evaluation methodologies

People perceive and appreciate landscapes in many different ways. Approaches to landscape evaluation reflect this perception with a great variety of different methodologies having been used. They range from scenic approaches, such as that of Fines (1968), to those based more on physical rather than visual attributes, such as Linton (1968). In the former, where assessors mark views in the field on a 1 to 10 scale based on a set of photographs of standard landscapes previously calibrated by a sample of people,

Table 10.2 Goals, criteria and measures for the evaluation of threatened landscapes

Goals	Criterion	Measure, parameter
To maintain, or provide for, diverse ecosytems, biotopes, and landscapes – the greater the number of different indigenous artefacts, wildlife species, vegetation communities, etc., the more valuable	Diversity	The regional standard spectrum of differences; number of different cultural, biotic and abiotic features
To maintain, or preserve, typical ecosytems, biotopes and landscapes – the greater the number of characteristic groups of topography, land use, vegetation etc., the more valuable (the more familiar, or easily recognized) they are, cf. 'zonal vegetation'	Typicalness	The number and combinations of shared and essential features that make the area representative of the region to which it belongs
To maintain, or preserve, ecosystems, biotopes and landscapes in authentic, unimpaired conditions	Integrity	The completeness and effective functioning of features within a regional standard
To preserve rare species, biotopes and landscapes – the more regionally unusual, distinguished or unique landforms, plant communities, etc. are, the more valuable is the area containing them (also uniqueness of the area itself)	Rarity	The uniqueness and scarcity of individual features, landscapes

the emphasis throughout is on value judgements. More physical approaches relying on the survey of landform and land use are more objective, but still involve value judgements in the selection of attributes and the means of their aggregation.

Methodologies reflect both objectives and the background of those undertaking them. Wascher (1997) quotes Taylor *et al.* (1987): 'Many people in these areas, as well as those in other landscape study disciplines, tended to use their own disciplinary paradigms to develop tools to measure landscape aesthetics and other values. In short order a proliferation of landscape assessment techniques appeared based upon a number of different conceptual approaches.' This American study identified four main research paradigms: expert, psychophysical, cognitive, and experiential. 'In the expert paradigm, highly skilled observers such as landscape architects or ecologists do the assessments. In the psychophysical paradigm, landscape values seem to derive from the actions of landscape stimulus features on passive human respondents. In the cognitive paradigm, people tend to be seen as "thinkers" whose aesthetic values come from the way information is given meaning in the mind or through social processes. The experiential paradigm views people as active participants in the landscape, deriving their values from experience'.

A number of systems have been used for the assessment or evaluation of landscapes for different purposes (for example, Kaule 1968, Countryside Commission 1993). The most practically useful build upon parameters such as rarity, diversity, integrity and representativeness which have been successfully applied as criteria in the selection of nature reserves (Usher 1986, Spellerberg 1992), or for the identification of environmentally sensitive areas (Cook *et al.* 1992), and some incorporate elements of both scenic and physical approaches. Standardized methodologies need to be developed and widely accepted if the assessments, which will be required for political initiatives such as The European Landscape Convention, are to be effectively implemented. Wascher (1998) sets out some key landscape indicators (Table 10.3) and observes that:

> The development of agri-environmental indicators at the international level will require a great deal of data harmonisation and standardisation in order to allow proper management and interpretation. Though many OECD Member States control relatively large amounts of land-related data (e.g. on land use, land cover, topography, demography, infrastructure, biotopes, soils, climate, site designation), most of this data is still not accessible and operational at the international level. In terms of data harmonisation, the use of remote sensing data and the application of Geographic Information Systems (GIS) has gained world-wide increasing significance for monitoring state and changes in the environment. Up to the present time, the available capacities of interpreting and manipulating remote sensing data have only been partially exploited for policy implementation. Remote sensing data exists for some OECD countries and with CORINE land cover at the level of the European Union plus some accession states. Precise geographic identifications of land use structures, landscape elements, landforms,

patch sizes and socio-economic patterns provide a wealth of information that can be linked to other layers such as topography, climate, soil and vegetation data. While remote-sensing data does not cover all information needs, it should be considered as an important prerequisite when developing international indicators.

Monetary evaluations

Planners are not only interested in landscape evaluation as a means of comparing different landscapes with one another in order to decide on priorities for their protection, or to monitor change. In the zoning and control of development, sieve map and various potential surface analysis techniques stemming from McHarg (1969) are commonly employed in the attempt to ascertain which of a number of potential land uses might most appropriately occupy a particular piece of territory. Agricultural, sylvicultural, hydrological, recreational, wildlife and scenic values are commonly compared in this process. This evaluation is very different from each of the individual evaluations since it is not comparing like with like. A common denominator is therefore required and this usually is 'the mischievous quantifier', that is: money. In an unmoderated evaluation of this kind the potentially most lucrative land use

Table 10.3 Examples of indicators to assess the state and trends of landscapes according to function

Landscape function	Landscape areas	Landscape elements
Perception & culture	Openness versus closedness (proportion of cropland/grassland/ forests in %)	Geological formations (index)
	Spatial field pattern (ISU/AU)	Historical and cultural monuments (index)
	Land cover diversity (Shannon index)	Linear features (length of hedges, walls, fences, rivers, forest edges/AU)
	Boundaries I (length water/land)	
	Boundaries II (length between land cover types)	Punctual features (number of trees, ponds, monuments/AU)
	Naturalness (semi-natural + natural habitat types, % of AU)	Archaeological sites (number/AU)
	Habitat type of preference (% of AU)	
Ecology & environment	Water retention functions (% of AU)	Total number of species associated with agricultural land use/AU
	Water quality (index)	Number of protected species/AU
	Habitat diversity (Shannon index)	Linear features (length of hedges, walls, fences, rivers, forest edges/AU)
	Protected areas (% of AU)	
	Soil type	Punctual features (number of trees, ponds, monuments/AU)
	Geology	

AU = Area Unit
Source: Wascher 1998

will always succeed. Since wildlife and landscape values are difficult to assess in monetary terms they all too often lose out in these economically based decisions.

Attempts have thus been made to make monetary evaluations of wildlife and landscape. Some have been unashamedly arbitrary in simply converting numerical assessments of wildlife value into currency. More recent approaches attempt to use actual monetary measures or estimates. 'Travel cost methods' calculate how much how many people spend in reaching a site. 'Hedonic pricing' isolates the amenity component in the price of goods, for example, by surveying how much more than average houses with a beautiful view are priced. 'Contingent valuation' techniques use market research to estimate how much people are willing to pay for an amenity. All these methods can give some idea of the 'actual use value' of amenities. Only contingent valuation can give estimates of the 'option value' of the benefits of environmental goods at some future time, or of the 'existence value' of those such as whales, for example, which some people may never see yet still cherish.

Conclusion

Landscape evaluation is still a developing endeavour which presents many conceptual and practical problems. The fact that it is dependent, as an essential prerequisite, on standard landscape classification, which is itself also still developing, means that much more collaboration between researchers often working in different disciplines and countries is necessary. There is, however, little doubt of its importance and practical utility for a variety of purposes in landscape planning and management. It is difficult to see how landscape protection and sustainable use of the environment will be possible without it. One important reason for this is that, whilst the aim of a purely objective evaluation is probably unobtainable, systematic methodologies enable those involved to explain and justify them, while also enabling others to understand how decisions were made. This ability to stand exposure to public scrutiny is an increasingly vital part of the political process.

Chapter 11

European landscapes in transition: levels of intervention

D. M. Wascher

Introduction

Discovering appropriate ways of living in different landscapes has been the key to the rise of civilization. For millennia the development of human society has been a function of people's capacity to control their landscape of origin, civilization being fundamentally rooted in and moulded according to physical landscape characteristics. The technologically and economically advanced societies of Mesopotamia, for example, thrived upon a knowledge base that was intrinsically linked to the challenges of managing the landscape's complex and dynamic water systems. Mediterranean societies such as those of the Greeks and Romans, as well as most other more recent European cultures, have likewise been shaped by a variety of factors among which landscape characteristics are generally considered as highly influential. Failure to manage landscapes sustainably certainly appears to have been a key factor in the decline of many civilizations. Deforestation, desertification and salinization still threaten people's livelihoods in many parts of the world today. Progress in the fields of science, technology and trade has deepened the divide between the service function of landscapes and a society's overall socio-economic and environmental objectives. Large-scale and pervasive changes in landscape form and function are now achieved in a fraction of the time and effort necessary in the past. Maintaining cherished landscape features and traditional ways of rural life without fossilization and hardship presents a formidable challenge to policy-makers and planners.

Three levels of intervention could contribute towards a transition of European landscapes in the near future, namely:

- developing sustainable agriculture and forestry as a top-down driving force for maintaining high landscape values ('the economic transition');
- improving the international legal framework for landscape conservation and planning ('the policy transition');
- developing a model of society that is more deeply anchored in regional landscapes ('the socio-holistic transition').

All three transitions form complementary units for a common European future perspective on landscapes.

The economic transition

Because most European landscapes are farmed, agricultural policy and practice largely determines their nature. Farming may not feature in every landscape, but covering 51 per cent of EU territory, agriculture remains the main land use. It should be noted, however, that other sectors, such as forestry, tourism or traffic, offer other important challenges and opportunities for economic transitions. In a recent communication (CEC 1999) the European Commission Agriculture Directorate addressed explicitly the outstanding role of landscapes as both an environmental and socio-economic issue. Yet, although so socially and politically highly relevant, today's agricultural production plays only a marginal role in terms of most countries' GNP or employment rate. More than ever before, both European agriculture and its corresponding landscapes have become commodity items on the global market of free trade that is challenging the political agenda of the European Union and of their present and future members. In the age of globalization and information, the future perspectives of agricultural landscapes appear as increasingly uncertain. Monitoring changes in them is therefore of increasing urgency and importance and is being pursued through a number of European initiatives.

Even with only a basic knowledge of ecological and socio-economic issues related to agriculture, it is evident that there are causal links between soil types, land use, habitat quality, biodiversity and social appreciation. One could argue that it is enough to examine the individual components in order to understand the agri-environmental complex. The assumption underlying this approach (which can be described as vertical) is that if certain environmental targets (benchmarks) for each individual component, or some indicator of it, are met, this will automatically result in a positive state of the environment as a whole. However, given the definitions and objectives laid down in recent European policy documents such as Agenda 2000 (CEC 1998), the European Spatial Development Perspective and the Pan-European Biological and Landscape Diversity Strategy, the adequacy of an exclusively vertical approach must be doubted. Issues such as rural development, cultural landscapes and regional identity form a set of values that extend the concept of sustainability. What all these issues have in common is that socio-economic considerations play a vital role when defining environmental objectives.

As a spin-off from work on agri-environmental indicators (Wascher, in press), the European Commission has provided input to OECD initiatives through a paper on 'Indicators for agricultural landscapes', taking into account the results and outputs of two Eurostat workshops on landscape indicators held in 1998. As a result, OECD has nominated three umbrella indicators, addressing diversity, cultural and conservation aspects, as part of future agri-environmental assessments.

Following these initiatives, the European Commission has continued with further elaborations of its own policy evelution programmes by establishing landscapes as one of five headline environmental indicators and by setting up new landscape-oriented incentive schemes for environmentally friendly farming practices. The transition towards more sustainable forms of agriculture thus has a clear focus on the landscape dimension. It can be expected that the implementation of Agenda 2000 will prompt member states also to develop national policies in support of landscapes. Some of the opportunities and challenges this presents are discussed in Chapter 12.

The policy transition

Until recently environmental protection and management focused largely on seemingly separate, disparate areas of concern such as biodiversity, beautiful scenery, historical monuments, recreation areas and traditional ways of life. While there has been some overlap, these concerns have been largely addressed in discrete compartments, usually by different agencies. Most conservation effort has arguably been directed at protected areas of various kinds where the protection of wildlife, sometimes coupled with recreation, has been the paramount objective (Table 11.1). In National Parks the internationally recognized definition adopted by IUCN specifically excludes human activities:

A National Park (IUCN Category II) is a relatively large area . . .

- where one or several ecosystems are not materially altered by human exploitation and occupation, where plant and animal species, geomorphological sites and habitats are of special scientific, educative and recreative interest or which contains a natural landscape of great beauty; and
- where the highest competent authority of the country has taken steps to prevent or to eliminate as soon as possible exploitation or occupation in the whole area and to enforce effectively the respect of ecological, geomorphological or aesthetic features which have led to its establishment; and
- where visitors are allowed to enter, under special conditions, for inspiration, educative, cultural and recreative purposes.

(Lucas 1992)

Native Americans were resettled when one of the earliest national parks, Yosemite, was established, and similar attitudes have continued to dominate much thinking about national parks throughout the world. In the IUCN scheme, lived-in landscapes are relegated to a somewhat second-rate category of Protected Landscape (IUCN Category V):

to maintain nationally significant natural landscapes which are characteristic of the harmonious interaction of People and Land, while providing opportunities for public enjoyment through recreation and tourism within the normal life-style and economic activity of these areas.

(Lucas 1992)

Table 11.1 IUCN Categories of Protected Areas (Summary)

    I.   Scientific Reserve/Strict Nature Reserve

    II.   National Park

    III.   Natural Monument/Natural Landmark

    IV.   Nature Conservation Reserve/Managed Reserve/Wildlife Sanctuary

    V.   Protected Landscape or Seascape

    VI.   Resource Reserve–Interim Conservation Unit

    VII.   Natural Biotic Area/Anthropological Reserve

    VIII.   Multi-use Management Areas/Managed Resource Areas

Source: IUCN 1990

Although the IUCN Scheme, adopted as Resolution 1 at the Tenth General Assembly of IUCN in Delhi in 1969, specifically requested that cultural landscapes should not be designated as national parks, several countries, notably England and Wales, have done so. Others, such as France, have placed considerable emphasis on the designation of cultural landscape as Parc Régional Naturel, with socio-economic objectives taking high priority.

In recent years the old, purist view of national parks has come to be increasingly questioned on ecological, geographical, practical managerial and socio-economic grounds, with larger landscape units coming to be seen as the key to integrated, holistic, sustainable environmental planning and management (Chapter 12). The increasing significance of landscapes as a policy issue at the European level has resulted in the need for more information on the geographical distribution and typology of these landscapes. Policy implementation requires knowledge about the exact location, extension and characteristics of landscapes that become the subject of policy interest. Despite a number of encouraging research activities in the field of landscape ecology and geography, there is still a lack of widely recognized, standardized landscape typology and mapping that can find useful application in the policy field. While a number of useful landscape typologies and maps have been developed at the national level, European approaches towards landscape mapping are still facing severe problems in terms of scale, accuracy and policy relevance. Policy relevance depends on the degree to which the level of scale corresponds with the level of actual decision-making. For general assessments it might suffice to operate at the level of landscape regions, while more specific questions of policy implementation at the national and regional level might require differentiating between landscape types or units (see Chapter 3).

At the international and European levels a number of major new policy measures for improving a common understanding of the character and distribution of landscapes are being implemented.

The World Heritage Convention

At the global level, UNESCO started in 1993 to inscribe cultural landscapes on the World Heritage List, following the revision of criteria for cultural properties adopted at the sixteenth session of the World Heritage Committee in Santa Fe (1992). The designation of UNESCO cultural landscape sites is very much based on the notion of 'cultural tradition', and specifically as examples of outstanding land use (see Paragraph 24(a) in UNESCO's Operational Guidelines, 1995). Hence, the shaping of landscape by agriculture, for example, the citrus terraces in the Hiroshima Prefecture in Japan, or the Upper St. John Valley in the United States, is one of the criteria for qualifying for the World Heritage List.

Pan-European Biological and Landscape Diversity Strategy

The Action Plan on European Landscapes is part of the Pan-European Biological and Landscape Diversity Strategy (PEBLDS) (Council of Europe, UNEP & ECNC 1995) that has been signed by 55 European countries and is presently under implementation. The central objective of Action Theme 4 is to promote actively the landscape concept as an opportunity to address all those pressing landscape issues which are complementary to, but at the European level not sufficiently affected by, classical nature conservation approaches. Rather than being limited to area protection, the landscape concept offers integrative, preventive and proactive tools to counteract multi-dimensional environmental pressures and to initiate large-scale mitigation and restoration processes. Recent achievements of implementing the Action Plan on landscapes were the development of a landscape assessment procedure with special focus on driving forces (Klijn *et al.* 1999) at a European Workshop on Landscape and Sustainability (Wascher 2000), and the first phase of developing a more detailed approach towards landscape mapping at the European level (Vervloet 2000).

The Draft European Landscape Convention

Since 1995, the Congress of Local and Regional Authorities of Europe (CLRAE) at the Council of Europe is leading the technical procedures to develop a European Landscape Convention. This convention is meant to apply to the entire European territory of the 'Parties' (member states) and covers natural, rural, urban and peri-urban areas (Council of Europe 1997). While referring to both cultural and environmental considerations, the draft European Landscape Convention is based upon two particular principles. First, the scope of the draft Convention covers not only remarkable landscapes but also ordinary ones; and second, it emphasizes the active role for citizens in decisions regarding their landscapes. In order to achieve these innovative principles in an appropriate way, the draft Convention provides for the fact that each signatory state would commit to guaranteeing the protection, management and development of these landscapes through the implementation of national measures and through the organization of co-operation at European level.

Legislative programmes related to landscapes

The UNESCO *Operational Guidelines* (WHC/2/Revised 1995, Paragraph 38), state:

'Cultural landscapes often reflect specific techniques of sustainable land use, considering the characteristics and limits of the natural environment they are established in, and the specific spiritual relation to nature. The continued existence of traditional forms of land use supports biological diversity in many regions of the world.'

The European Commission's *Agenda 2000* states:

'For centuries Europe's agriculture has performed many functions in the economy and the environment and has played many roles in society and in caring for the land. That is why it is vital, as the Luxembourg European Council concluded in December 1997, that multi-functional agriculture must develop throughout Europe, including those regions facing particular difficulties. In connection with Agenda 2000 and its implementation, care will accordingly need to be taken to provide proper compensation for natural constraints and disadvantages.'

'The fundamental difference between the European model and that of our major competitors lies in the multi-functional nature of Europe's agriculture and the part it plays in the economy and the environment, in society and in preserving the landscape, hence the need to maintain farming throughout Europe and to safeguard farmers' incomes.' (CEC 1998).

The European Commission's *European Spatial Development Perspective (ESDP)* identifies in Chapter III under 'Policy aims':

'The diversity of cultural landscapes in Europe is a precious heritage. They provide a visible regional identity and are a record of history and an expression of human interaction with nature. Efforts made to maintain regional landscapes and their beauty do not prevent or hamper economic stimulus.'

The document lists the following policy options: 'Longer-term conservation and management of landscapes of cultural and historical importance through sound land-use planning and management; creative rehabilitation of landscapes degraded by different human activities; preservation of characteristic landscapes in areas threatened by agricultural abandonment' (CEC 1998).

UNEP/Council of Europe's *Pan-European Strategy for Biological and Landscape Diversity* names under Action Theme 4 on the Conservation of landscapes the following challenges: 'To prevent further deterioration of the landscapes and their associated cultural and geological heritage in Europe, and to preserve their beauty and identity. To correct the lack of integrated perception of landscapes as a unique mosaic of cultural, natural and geological features and to establish a better public and policy-maker awareness and more suitable protection status for these features throughout Europe' (Council of Europe 1995).

Landscapes as addressed by national legislation and policies

Many countries have some form of legislation which affects landscape either directly, for example, through protection of features, or indirectly, mainly through restrictions for urban expansion or for agricultural practices. Prieur (1997) has reviewed national laws relating to landscape in the member states of The Council of Europe and concludes that landscape has been legally regulated in three main ways:

- under legislation on historic monuments and sites, emphasizing landscape as the reflection of beauty and aesthetic value;
- under legislation on protection of the environment, emphasizing landscape as the reflection of a vision of outstanding natural spaces and environments, given form in parks and reserves;
- under legislation on land use and town planning, emphasizing landscape as the reflection of both a natural and cultural vision of space and recognizing the intrinsic value of even ordinary landscapes.

In a review of landscape policies and initiatives in European Union countries, Wascher (2000) concluded that, though the number, extent and enforcement of such policies varies considerably, key objectives include:

- protection of agricultural landscapes, habitats and biotopes and (singular) features;
- control/prohibition of certain types of agricultural practices, as agriculture has to perform economic, environmental and social functions, such as the preservation of landscapes;
- schemes providing farmers, foresters or other land managers with positive economic incentives for adopting a particular form of land management;
- the cultural, scenic, ecological and historical importance of landscapes shall be maintained through sound land-use planning (including urban development on farmland, afforestation programmes, watershed schemes, etc.);
- landscapes which have been degenerated or degraded, due to agricultural intensification or abandonment, shall be (creatively) restored.

Comparison between the national approaches showed that virtually all initiatives in this field are relatively new and that many have not been fully implemented yet. This is not only due to the relative novelty of the landscape concept entering the field of environmental assessment, but also due to the fact that systematic landscape survey, evaluation, monitoring and the use of indicator applications are relatively underdeveloped approaches at the national level. Given the 'frontier' character of the task, impressive scope and depth has been developed for some of these approaches. Besides a number of commonalities, however, there are also clear differences in terms of the underlying methodological rationales, the sequence of activities and the use of assessment tools. Landscape character and landscape functions are treated with much detail by the Scandinavian, Italian and British assessment programmes. The Scandinavian systems combine sampling devices with large-scale area analysis of agricultural statistics, examining the links between landscape changes over time (baseline data) and farming activities. The identification of distinct landscape units plays an important role in the United Kingdom, Germany, Italy and Japan. Driving forces in the form of rural processes, as examined by the Dutch Spatial Planning Agency discussed in the next chapter, are also given high priority in France. However, since land-use data still play an important role in many European countries, the role of landscape conservation must be considered relatively high with regard to surface area under environmental protection (Table 11.2). This is especially the case in most western and central European countries. However, the actual legislation and financial support for landscape protection areas is relatively modest, compared to other types of protected areas, such as national parks and nature reserves.

The socio-holistic transition

Whether at local, regional, national or international scale, landscapes express the uniqueness and identity of each place (the 'genius loci'), reflecting both natural and cultural history of a territory at a given time (Gulinck & Mugica, in press). Landscape can thus be considered as a horizontal system that can provide the infrastructure or linkages to all other environmental media and

Table 11.2 Landscape Protection compared with Nature Conservation in European countries with averages for bio-geographic regions (percentage of total surface area)

Country	Nature conservation	Landscape conservation	Country	Nature conservation	Landscape conservation
Mediterranean region:			**North–west European region:**		
Spain	0.3	7.8	Germany	1.8	24.9
Portugal	1.6	4.2	France	0.8	8.9
Italy	0.9	3.0	Ireland	6.3	0.0
Greece	0.5	1.1	United Kingdom	5.3	12.7
Regional average	*0.8*	*4.0*	Luxembourg	0.0	37.7
			The Netherlands	3.7	2.8
Alpine region:			Belgium	0.6	2.2
Austria	5.7	18.2	Denmark	2.3	22.4
Switzerland	2.4	14.9	*Regional average*	*2.6*	*14.0*
Regional average	*4.1*	*16.6*			
			Scandinavian region:		
Central–east European region:			Finland	2.3	0.1
Hungary	3.1	8.3	Norway	10.8	1.4
Poland	0.5	9.1	Sweden	2.7	2.7
Regional average	*1.8*	*8.7*	Iceland	1.6	6.3
			Regional average	*4.4*	*2.6*

Source: Wascher 1995

systems. The concept of landscape hence is practicable when developing a holistic approach. The availability and character of natural resources are the key determining factors for the type and extent of human activities. The natural environmental conditions of a specific region hence provide the basis for the type of land-use activities that can be considered sustainable, meaning that they are in adequate balance with the production and self-regenerating capacities of that region. Landscape planning is essentially concerned with appropriately matching land use with land capability.

As depicted in Fig. 11.1, natural landscapes hold a central position and are considered to be the key factor in determining land use. The underlying assumption is that the character of each type of natural landscape is defined by a set of criteria such as geomorphology, climate, hydrology and topography that also control the land-use activities and production regimes that can be considered as a sustainable optimum in that set of circumstances. As natural landscapes are described in terms of regionally specific (native) habitats and species, coherence is achieved when agricultural land use reflects and allows the presence and function of these and other natural bio-physical factors. Because modern technology is powerful enough to override natural constraints, it allows in principle almost any form of land use regardless of natural conditions. Any sustainable agri-environmental scheme consonant with landscape characteristics inevitably therefore requires a fundamental reassessment of existing agricultural land use.

The close link between land use and social appreciation is recognized by the visual characteristics of both the natural and cultural landscapes. This relation is marked by the functional relation that is indicated by the central role of land use between the natural and cultural aspects of the landscape. The arrows are supposed to illustrate the direct and indirect impact of the

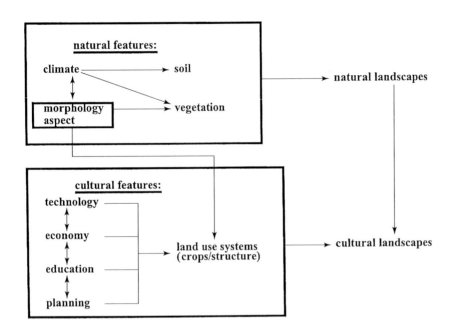

11.1 Natural and cultural components of landscapes

Source: Jongman 1996

natural conditions on the character of the cultural landscapes and hence on landscape perception. Even in an area that is entirely under agricultural land use, the natural conditions in terms of topography, geomorphology and hydrology will be a visible component, especially, but not only, on a large scale (for example, from a bird's eye view).

Figure 11.1 also indicates that the system biodiversity and the media of soil, water and air have close direct interrelations with land use as well as with the conditions defined by the natural landscape character. The scheme portrays impact to be strong from natural landscape aspects on land use and subsequently on cultural landscapes, but weaker from natural landscape on cultural landscapes as cultural structures dominate landscape aspects in the European context. The scheme is hence less idealized but reflects actual environmental conditions.

Integrated environmental reporting

Since the first pan-European environmental report, *Europe's Environment – The Dobris Assessment* (Stanners & Bourdeau 1995), was published it has become evident that the greatly increasing availability of data does not always translate into better public and policy information on cross-sectoral issues such as sustainability, ecosystem health and land-use trends. It is important to leave the purely media-oriented debate behind and start developing a more systematic approach to land-use and environmental issues. When shifting from vertical analysis towards a more horizontal synthesis, high emphasis must be placed on developing adequate geographic references that reflect ecologically coherent units. In order to provide a high level of transparency and differentiation, new approaches for environmental reporting and policy control must be based on integrated cause–effect mechanisms that are well monitored. The development of Europe-wide harmonized common databases such as a common classification of European landscapes is one of the key prerequisites.

This chapter is based on the author's report to the UNESCO workshop on agri-environmental indicators (Wascher 1998).

Chapter 12

Managing old landscapes and making new ones

B. H. Green and W. Vos

Introduction

The very gradual development over millennia of farming, forestry and other rural land uses in the post-glacial landscapes of Europe has permitted the largely spontaneous colonization of landscapes by native plant and animal species. Thus anthropogenic pastures, meadows and heaths cleared from the original forest cover came to be composed of plants and animals colonizing them from naturally open habitats such as dunes, cliffs, marshes and woodland glades. Planted arable crops, vineyards, olive groves, orchards and timber tree plantations were also colonized by wild native species. Some of these species have evolved distinct ecotypes, or even new species, in these human-made and human-maintained agro-ecosystems. Some of the latter have developed higher levels of biodiversity than the natural ecosystems from which they originated. Many species, such as the green-winged orchid, blue butter-flies, skylarks and lapwings, must have developed far larger populations in such managed ecosystems than they ever did in those which were truly natural. A traditional mixture of croplands, pastures and trees was the backbone of these landscapes and these three kinds of land use occurred at field level (mixed cropping, rotations), farm enterprise level (mixed farming) and landscape level (zonations based on land capabilities). Practically every place and every tree played multiple roles within these systems. Cultural landscapes composed of aggregations of semi-natural managed ecosystems are greatly cherished not only for their biodiversity, but also for their landscape beauty, historical associations and the opportunities they offer for informal outdoor recreation.

The familiarity of this situation to the European should not obscure the fact that such rich cultural landscapes, in general, do not occur in those parts of the world where human intervention is more recent. Even in the seemingly comparable and superficially similar temperate parts of eastern North America or New Zealand, forest clearance and farming has resulted not in rich semi-natural ecosystems of native species, but in species-poor examples of meadows and pastures dominated by common European grasses and herbs.

In these other parts of the world the evolution of species on very infertile soils seems to have made them less effective competitors than European species evolved for millennia alongside farming. Wherever European farmland species have been introduced they have come to play a major role in the farmed landscapes of temperate zones.

Sustainable land use

European cultural landscapes therefore provide unusual examples of the way in which ecosystem production can be sustainably exploited while maintaining indigenous biodiversity and other amenities which allow multipurpose use. The maintenance of these environmental qualities was, however, in most cases an unintended by-product of an agriculture that was not capable of controlling all production factors, so that outputs as well as inputs were low. In traditional systems the organization of space was strongly related to local chemical, energy and water supplies for agricultural production. Crop rotation and inputs from nearby land, such as manure from livestock, mulch, charcoal and firewood from forests and fertilizing by innundation, were the key means of resource capture. In this way, and with the collection of fruits, mushrooms, honey, game, tree leaves, twigs and bark as livestock fodder, apparently 'unused' nature was integrated into the land-use systems. The basic trinity of arable, grassland and trees, arranged at different scales, determined the nature of landscapes for many centuries or even millennia (Vos, Austad & Pinto Correia 1994).

Environmental extremes were addressed with local solutions: lowland dyke systems and windmills were used to safeguard and reclaim waterlogged land; stands of elms for leaves and birches for bark as animal fodder were exploited in areas with a long annual snow cover; transhumance around the Mediterranean was a response to periodic droughts in the lowlands and snow in the mountains. Differences in local resources also contributed strongly to landscape differentiation: location determined whether wood, peat, wind, or stream water were used as sources of energy supply; differences in available materials determined the nature of field boundaries as hedges, stone walls, fences, or canals and ditches; differences in available building materials meant that vernacular archiecture was generally made from what it stood on, or was surrounded by, whether stone, clay/brick, loam, or timber and reeds. It was a perfect fit in the landscape; reflecting the spirit of the place by literally growing out of the same materials.

In general, these traditional systems reached their optimum in the second half of the nineteenth century. By that time livestock had become a central component, not only for their meat, milk, wool and hides, but also for their manure and animal power for transport. In many cases these systems kept a balance between population numbers and farm production, often reaching steady states of land use and land cover. In that sense they could be sustainable for a long time. But not always, especially when disrupted by catastrophies, or the effects of wars and epidemics. The amount of production which can be exploited while keeping biodiversity and amenity within acceptable limits is restricted. Species-rich ecosystems tend to be inherently unproductive. Traditional land uses, constrained by low fertility, waterlogging, difficult terrain and other limiting factors inherent in the land and by the limits of human labour, could not generally exceed the modest sustainable yield available from them without causing environmental deterioration. Such over-exploitation did occur. Some north-west European heathlands were overgrazed to mobile sand dunes. On Crete, the forested mountains were nearly completely cleared after the Ottoman occupation (1669) and are now still largely bare rock. Lowland Christian Cretan farmers withdrew into the mountains with their flocks, causing overgrazing and fires. Even before Plato (429–348 BC) the land near Athens was so much degraded by overgrazing and burning that he worried about the resulting erosion.

Modern farming, forestry and other land uses are not so constrained as the traditional ones. Machinery and chemicals can overcome all the old limiting factors. Given the necessary fossil fuel subsidy, modern farming systems have proved sustainable in terms of yield, but not in terms of maintaining the high biodiversity, amenity and historical features which were an integral part of the older systems. The high fertility and effective control of pests and diseases needed for high production dictates monocultures of vigorous species which outcompete and displace most other species. The biodiversity and amenity produced automatically by old systems of farming are now seen as 'externalities' – non-market goods which must be especially managed and paid for.

As farming and other rural land uses intensified, and spatial segregation and specialization progressed, biodiversity and amenity were initially provided for outside the production system as isolated parks and reserves, managed exclusively for recreation and wildlife. Integrated multifunctional rural systems were replaced by more specialized ones. More recently the inability of such isolated sites to maintain viable populations of plants and animals and the difficulties in managing them independently from the rest of the country-side has led to the additional strategy of paying farmers to work in more environmentally friendly, but inevitably less productive, ways and improving connectivity by creating habitat corridors. Since appropriate human activity plays an undeniable role in generating the semi-natural and more production-oriented agro-ecosystems that provide characteristic and high levels of biodiversity and amenity, it is obvious that it must continue in order to maintain these levels. Complete landscapes can perhaps only be maintained by this approach; they are generally too large and their ecological and socio-economic linkages too complex to be sustained as island parks or reserves. Sustainability is perhaps only a meaningful concept at the landscape scale; it is probably impossible to manage every hectare of land sustainably, but with different areas being managed at different intensities, sustainability of the overall landscape complex may be achieved.

Farmers as landscape managers

As the case studies in Part Two show, traditionally managed landscapes are being lost everywhere; mostly through either agricultural intensification or abandonment (Fig. 12.1). Since 1985 (Council Regulation 797/85) the

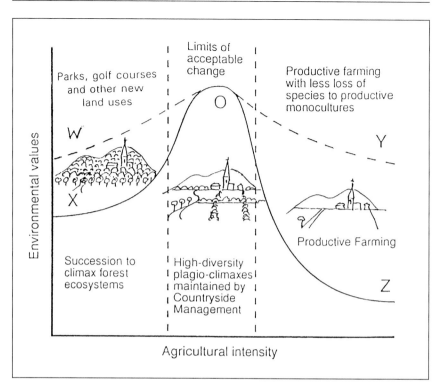

12.1 Cultural landscape dynamics

Table 12.1 Measures in 158 programmes proposed by member states under Regulation 2078/92

Measure	Article	Objective			
		Market organization; reduction of surpluses	Environment; less pollution; protection nat. resources	Landscape preservation	Prevention agricultural decline and hazards
Reduction of inputs	(2.1.a)	X	X		
Organic farming	(2.1.a)	X	X		
Extensification	(2.1.a)	X	X	X	
Convert arable into grassland	(2.1.b)	X	X		
Reduction of livestock density	(2.1.c)	X	X		
Environmental practice	(2.1.d)	X	X	X	X
Maintainance of landscape	(2.1.d)			X	X
Rearing animals in danger	(2.1.d)		X		X
Upkeep of abandoned land	(2.1.e)		X	X	X
20 year set-aside	(2.1.f)	X	X	X	X
Manage land for public access	(2.1.g)			X	
Training/demonstration projects	(2.2)	X	X	X	X

Source: De Putter 1995

142

European Community has addressed this problem by enabling farmers to take advantage of a variety of agri-environment schemes whereby they are paid to farm in ways more appropriate for the protection of wildlife and amenity (CEC 1993). The 1992 Agri-environmental Regulation (2078/92) is the basis for most of the current measures. An analysis of 158 submitted programmes under this Regulation shows that the proposed measures cover a wide range (Table 12.1) (De Putter 1995).

While, in principle, such schemes seem to offer an effective way of maintaining traditional landscapes, in practice their impact so far has been small in most European countries compared with the massive impact of the Common Agricultural Policy of the EU on agricultural markets and commodity prices. Only a tiny fraction of farm production subsidies have been switched to environmental management schemes and the voluntary uptake of such schemes by farmers has for the most part been disappointing. The transfer of more money to environmental management is now nonetheless seen by many, including farmers, as the only way in which some state subsidy of the industry can continue in the face of trade liberalization. It is also seen as perhaps the only way in which many small marginal farmers, mostly involved in livestock husbandry in mountain areas, can be guaranteed future livelihoods.

This, as yet, has still to be reflected in any significant way in proposals to reform the Common Agricultural Policy. While some member states have reallocated significant amounts of production subsidy to environmental payments (in Austria it is some 30 per cent with 70 per cent of farmland under agri-environment agreements; in The Netherlands some 20 per cent of all state management costs for forest, nature and landscape is paid under agreements with farmers), most have not done so. Presently only some four per cent of agricultural subsidies are directed to environmental management schemes in the European Union with 17 per cent of land under agreements.

While agri-environment schemes have undoubtedly slowed down and in some cases reversed the attrition of the environment by intensive agriculture, more money for them would not necessarily solve the problem entirely. There are several reasons to suppose that the confidence of many farmers and environmentalists that it would do so may be misplaced.

First, the demography of farmers and their inheritors is not favourable. Over half the farmers in the EU are over 55 years old, and nearly half have no successor (CEC 1988). In mountainous regions and in the south, farm succession is even less assured (Baldock *et al.* 1996). Marginal farming, particularly of livestock in the hills, though so important in maintaining open landscapes and seemingly such an attractive way of life when seen by most visitors in the summer, is in fact a very hard way of making a living (Poole *et al.* 1998). Young people are moving out of such farming everywhere into urban and other easier lifestyles. Between 1965 and 1985 the number of farmers of the twelve EU countries decreased from 15 to 8 million: from 17 per cent to 6 per cent of the professional population, with only one out of three being a full-time farmer. Some back-migration, especially of hobby farmers and other part-timers, is in places to some extent compensating for this, but without an adequate work force such farmlands must either pass to forestry, or other uses, or be abandoned. This has already happened to a surprising extent in Europe, though not yet generally to the extent in the East Coast States of the USA, where, in the last 100 years, much in the last 50 years, vast tracts of country have changed from 80 per cent farmland and 20 per cent forest to the reverse (CEC 1988, Bignal & McCracken 1996). In limited parts of Europe comparable proportions of agricultural land have been abandoned, mostly after World War II, especially in the mountain areas of Southern Europe (Vos & Stortelder 1992, Bethe & Bolsius 1995, Baldock *et al.* 1996).

Second, the continuity of subsidies for landscape management by farmers is not guaranteed. It seems unlikely that a large-scale continuation of subsidies with environmental rather than production objectives will be acceptable under international trade agreements. Some further switching of subsidy funds may be acceptable, but not of the larger part of the entire billions of ECU production support. Countries such as Australia and New Zealand have long removed all their subsidies to farming, yet have to compete in world markets. The exposure of New Zealand farmers to world prices since 1984 has not led to predicted rural collapse, but reduced land prices, easier entry of young farmers into the industry, diversified cropping patterns, lower sheep numbers, more forestry on marginal farmland, more biodiversity and reduced food prices (Harvey 1997, Stephenson 1997, Green 2000).

Third, no form of subsidized low-intensity farming is able to compete financially as a land use with strong urban, industrial or recreation claims. The pressure on the land by the latter forms of land use, like in the urbanized regions in north-west Europe, is frequently so great that only extremely industrialized forms of agriculture (glasshouse vegetable production, bio-industry) are competitive enough. No subsidies for any form of low-intensity farming will stop urban or industrial expansion.

Finally, it surely has to be accepted that, even were there sufficient labour and money, the entire countryside cannot be made into a museum of ersatz landscapes where a hundred years of agricultural technological progress is abandoned and traditional techniques frozen forever in an unchanging time warp. This might conceivably be possible if all competitors in world markets were to accept the same limitations, but that is highly unlikely because they do not enjoy the same benefits of cultural landscapes as is the case in Europe. Some representative landscapes may be able to be maintained by this means, but not the entire countryside.

An environmental market for post-modern landscapes?

Increasing consumer demand for traditional foods produced in traditional ways may, to some extent, help to maintain farmers as landscape managers. Consumers now expect from farmers a broader spectrum of old and new products and services than just bulk biomass production. Not only more traditional foods, but also foods with a strong local identity, health foods, gourmet snacks, perhaps to be tasted and bought at the farm and with a certification that sometimes gives extremely high added-value. Appellation and quality assurance labelling is moving from cheeses and wines to a much wider range of products. The opportunity to camp, walk, ride, cycle; to be guided in climbing and skiing; to 'produce' clean water; to maintain old buildings, walls, terracettes, archaeological sites, dykes, water systems, paths and roads are all now services sought from farmers (Vos *et al.* 1998). Moreover consumers want a healthy, safe and attractive environment with a rich natural image and artefacts that make the shared, common history readable. Many of a growing urban population which is becoming ever richer, at least in north, north-west and central Europe, seem to be willing to pay substantial amounts for these specialized niche products and services of localized provenance. This has long been the case in France, where consumers are prepared to spend a high proportion of their disposable income on specialized foods. Such products demand and command premium prices, generally being produced more labour-intensively and aimed at the more wealthy market sectors. Whether they ever prove able to seize a sufficiently large sector of the market to have a significant effect on the viability of traditional farming systems must depend on their ability to price competitively against more conventionally produced foodstuffs and on the willingness of enough consumers to pay whatever premiums are necessary. The growth of the organic food sector is a promising sign.

The guaranteed prices and markets of the Common Agricultural Policy, with all production, including surpluses, being bought into intervention has, unfortunately, insulated farmers from their markets and atrophied to a certain extent the marketing skills of agricultural producers in at least a large part of the European countryside. The vertical integration of food production and marketing with retailers controlling, indeed often owning and managing farmland, may, however, offer the best prospect for low-output, high-value foodstuffs produced in environmentally friendly ways. Such businesses are very sensitive to consumer demands. Many supermarkets already operate such quality assurance schemes, monitoring all stages in the food production, processing and marketing chain. Through very large-scale operations, including large farms, the economies of scale may help lower prices to levels which will greatly widen the market sector. This may not help small farmers, but it may increase the extent of land which is sensitively farmed. The future of small farmers probably lies in part-time and hobby farming. Loss of small farmers may not be as damaging to the environment as commonly imagined; for small farmers often seem to farm in environmentally friendly ways largely by default rather than intent, lacking the resources to farm more intensively (Potter & Lobley 1992).

The future of farming

Since agriculture occupies so much of the land, most of it hard won from the wild over centuries, the presumption is that it will continue to do so.

> Sufficient numbers of farmers must be kept on the land. There is no other way to preserve the natural environment, traditional landscapes and a model of agriculture based on the family farm as favoured by society generally. (CEC 1988)

12.2   The valley of the River Stour at Wye in Kent, England

A polarized landscape of modern agriculture, with intensive arable cultivation and dairy grazings on the fertile brickearth soils of the alluvial terraces of the river contrasting with semi-abandoned calcareous grasslands in the foreground on the escarpment slope of the hills of the North Downs. On the better farmland the removal of hedgerows has created large fields by the amalgamation of smaller ones, turning a Kampen-like landscape into open Champion. Some attempts have been made to ameliorate the loss of tree cover by plantings in waste corners and around buildings, supported by agri-environment schemes. On the steep slopes of the escarpment species-rich plant and invertebrate communities were formerly maintained by extensive sheep grazing with the flocks folded onto the lowland fields at night to fertilize them. This is no longer economic and most of these infertile hill grazings have either been left to scrub over or have been agriculturally improved with herbicides and fertilizers, increasing their production at the expense of their biodiversity. (Photograph: B Green)

There is, however, considerable overcapacity in European Union agriculture, which was an important reason for the switching of some production subsidies to environmental schemes. Some studies have suggested that potential surplus production is enormous and that as much as 80 per cent of farmland could come out of production, and yet self-sufficiency in food could be maintained by 2015 if the remaining farmland were allocated the best-suited sites and very intensively managed (NSCGP 1992). The accession of Eastern European Countries into the European Union will greatly increase food production capacity. With the liberalization of trade there might be great potential for Europe to increase its food exports. While overall world food security is probably not as threatened by population growth as pessimists foresee, the feeding of some countries, especially those in Africa, would seem likely to depend upon Europe joining North America as a major exporter of foodstuffs (Dyson 1996). If food supplies do come under pressure, most of the demand will probably be for grains which produce more food energy per unit area and unit cost than animal products. While, therefore, forecasts of vast areas being released from farming seem unlikely, the existing polarization of agriculture, with more intensive crop production on the better land and marginal grazing lands being managed less intensively, or abandoned, would seem likely to continue.

Apart from an 'external market', all people with any kind of means of production also have an 'internal market' that may guide their decisions. This is especially evident for food production in traditional subsistence households. Some imponderable functions which may influence the decisions of owners and tenants are respect, private or family identification with the land or estate and long-term investments. For these reasons they may choose to stay on the land in spite of what seems wise from a strict economic point of view. The land(scape) of the farmers and foresters has, however, also imponderable functions for broader groups in society. They may identify themselves with the natural or cultural heritage of 'their' territory, even if it is owned by somebody else. For these reasons they select their political parties, fund nature conservation movements, work as volunteers in landscape management, and buy specific regional products. For the natural and cultural heritage of 'their' society they will even start a war. Landscapes reflect who people are and what they are, and therefore they invest in them. Contrariwise, alienation from the land and its identity makes people not willing to invest in it and instead they will abandon it. Therefore the involvement of farmers, as well as nature conservationists, recreation enterpreneurs and all other groups engaged in a particular region, is an important condition for a balanced decision-making on future landscapes. In The Netherlands in the past decade a large number of so-called Environmental Associations, bringing together these groups, have developed with subsidies from national and regional governments. They have strongly stimulated different forms of an economically sound multifunctional agriculture (Vos *et al.* 1998).

New lives, new landscapes

Substantial changes in European rural land use took place in the second part of the twentieth century, and recreation and tourism are now a much more important base to the rural economy than agriculture in many European mountain and coastal areas. New leisure landscapes such as golf courses, equestrian centres, center parks and community forests are the twentieth century equivalents of hunting lodges which open up the countryside to a much wider selection of people, particularly those from urban areas. Some of them, such as golf courses, have been subject to similar accusations of narrow exclusivity in their usage as has hunting in some countries. Golf courses have also been criticized for being very artificial landscapes. In reality they are either modelled on sand dune ecosystems where the game began, or represent a kind of mechanically maintained wood pasture, where people chase small white balls rather than deer. New kinds of land use create new kinds of landscapes and those demanded and generated by an increasingly urban society are likely to be very different from those of the old rural society as growing conflicts over access to private land, animal welfare and transport networks are already beginning to reveal.

Coppiced forestlands, wood pastures, downlands, heathlands and *dehesas* were the incidental products of a rural industrial society. Only a few of the new urban-centred landscapes such as golf courses, reservoirs or the wet pits of the mineral extraction industries seem to be as congenial for wildlife or leisure as earlier rural industrial landscapes; they are certainly richer than most modern croplands. These new agricultural landscapes and the slag heaps, quarries and slurry beds of the extractive industries offer stern challenges to those concerned with realizing some of their potential for amenity use. Countryside managers are rapidly improving techniques for habitat restoration and translocation to meet these challenges. While it should not be supposed that ecosystems which have taken centuries to develop can be instantly replaced or substituted, habitats of considerable amenity value can be created quite quickly.

In the past vast landscapes did not only evolve slowly through the sum of the individual management decisions of numerous farmers and landowners. Some were imposed more rapidly through being redesigned or created anew. In much of Britain the Parliamentary and other enclosures, taking place mainly between 1750 and 1850, transformed an open-field landscape into a planned rectangular layout of fields and farms. In The Netherlands sea defences, drainage and land reclamation from medieval times onwards, converted the estuaries of three great rivers and adjacent lakes and peatlands into the characteristic polder farmland of a nation state. In the USA in the 1930s depressed marginal farmers in the hills of West Virginia were resettled on better land and their pastures and orchards allowed to revert back to the wild. A new tourist access road, the Skyline Drive, was constructed for tourists. Now the beautiful second growth forests of Shenandoah National Park attract more visitors than almost all other national parks in the USA. The Dutch with, in the most recent Flevoland polder, the great Oostvaardersplassen reserve grazed by feral herds of wild cattle and deer and with plans for even more imaginative new landscapes, especially in the flood plains of the River Rhine and the River Meuse, are advanced in conceiving new landscapes specially designed to accommodate new lifestyles (Harms *et al.* 1993). The restructuring of large parts of Westfalen (Germany) after the winning of brown coal by the Rheinbraun company is another extremely spectacular recent landscape transformation. All around the Mediterranean coastal zones are being transformed dramatically into recreation landscapes that may very well be attractive, as the older ones along the French and Italian Riviera demonstrate. Likewise many extensive coniferous forest landscapes, such as those of the Black Forest, Les Landes and the Ardennes, as well as forested regions of Ireland and Scotland, have been made in the past 150 years.

There is enormous potential in Europe today for similar landscape transformations. Some innovative and imaginative approaches are being developed to explore alternative ways in which familiar landscapes might develop and to assess people's preferences for them (O'Riordan *et al.* 1993). Modern agriculture will not automatically deliver the landscapes rich in wildlife, scenic beauty and recreational opportunity that traditional agriculture did in the past. We may be able to maintain some of these old landscapes, with new roles for a multifunctional agriculture, but for the most part we have to conceive, design, create and maintain new landscapes fit for the social, economic and environmental needs of the twenty-first century.

References

Chapter 1

Aalen, F., Whelan, K. and Stout, M. (eds) (1997) *Atlas of the Irish Rural Landscape,* Cork and Toronto: Cork University Press and University of Toronto Press.

Birks, H.H., Birks, H.J., Kaland, P.E. and Moe, D. (eds) (1988) *The Cultural Landscape: Past, Present and Future,* Cambridge: Cambridge University Press.

Braudel, F. (1988) *The identity of France*, Vol. 1, *History and Environment,* London: Fontana, pp. 71–72.

Chapman, J. and Dolukhanov, P. (eds) (1997) *Landscapes in Flux: Central and Eastern Europe in Antiquity,* Oxford: Oxbow.

Claval, P. (1990) 'European rural societies and landscapes, and the challenge of urbanization and industrialization in the nineteenth and twentieth centuries'. In Sporrong, U. (ed.) *The Transformation of Rural Society, Economy and Landscape,* Department of Human Geography, Stockholm University.

Cooney, G. (2000) *Landscapes of Neolithic Ireland,* London: Routledge.

Cunliffe, B. (ed.) (1994) *Prehistoric Europe,* Oxford: Oxford University Press.

Fabech, C. and Ringtved, J. (1999) *Settlement and Landscape,* Hojbjerg: Jutland Archaeological Society.

Fleming, A. (1998) *Swaledale, Valley of the Wild River*, Edinburgh: Edinburgh University Press.

Grove, A. and Rackham, O. (2001) *The Nature of Mediterranean Europe: an Ecological History*, London: Yale University Press.

Harris, D. (ed.) (1996) *The Origins and Spread of Agriculture and Pastoralism in Eurasia,* London: University College London Press.

Helmfrid, S. (ed.) (1994) *Landscape and Settlements: National Atlas of Sweden,* Stockholm: SNA Publishing, pp. 28–29.

McNeill, J. (1992) *The Mountains of the Mediterranean World*, Cambridge: Cambridge University Press.

Nitz, H-J. (1998) 'The Slavic hamlet round a cult green as the precursor of the regular rundling of the medieval Frankish-German colonisation', *Erdkunde* 52, 144–162.

Pfeifer, G. (1956) 'The quality of peasant living in central Europe'. In Thomas, W. (ed.) *Man's Role in Changing the Face of the Earth*, Chicago: University of Chicago Press, pp. 240–277.

Pounds, N. (1979) *An Historical Geography of Europe, 1500–1840,* Cambridge: Cambridge University Press.

Pounds, N. (1985) *An Historical Geography of Europe, 1800–1914,* Cambridge: Cambridge University Press.

Rackham, O. (1986) *The History of the Countryside,* London: Phoenix, pp. 155–159.

Rackham, O. (1990) 'Ancient landscapes'. In Murray, O. and Price, S. (eds) *The Greek City from Homer to Alexander,* Oxford: Clarendon Press.

Raumolin, J. (1987) 'Swidden Cultivation', *Suomen Antropologi,* 4, special issue, Helsinki.

Runnels, C. (1995) 'Environmental degradation in ancient Greece', *Scientific American,* March, 72–75.

Ruskin, J. (1844) *The Stones of Venice,* Vol.2.

Russell, E. W. B. (1997). *People and the Land Through Time. Linking ecology and history,* New Haven: Yale University Press.

Sanders, W. and Webster, D. (1994) 'Preindustrial man and environmental degradation'. In Kim, K. and Weaver, R. (eds) *Biodiversity and Landscape,* Cambridge: Cambridge University Press, pp. 77–104.

Sereni, E. (1997) *History of the Italian Agricultural Landscape,* Princeton: Princeton University Press, pp. 32–34.

Stanners, D. and Bourdeau, P. (eds) (1995) *Europe's Environment: the Dobris Assessment,* Copenhagen: European Environment Agency, pp. 464–477.

Thompson, F.M.L. (1985) 'Towns, industry and the Victorian landscape'. In Woodell, S. (ed.) *The English Landscape. Past, Present and Future,* Oxford: Oxford University Press, pp. 168–187.

Ucko, P. and Layton, R. (eds) (1999) *The Archaeology and Anthropology of Landscape,* London and New York: Routledge.

Vervloet, Rennes and Spek (1996) 'Historical geography and integrated landscape research'. In Aalen, F. (ed) *Landscape Study and Management,* Dublin: Boole Press.

Wascher, D. (ed.) (2000) *Landscapes and Sustainability. Proceedings of European Workshop on Landscape Assessment as a Policy Tool,* Tilburg and Cheltenham: European Centre for Nature Conservation and The Countryside Agency.

Worster, D. (1988) *The Ends of the Earth: Perspectives on Modern Environmental History,* Cambridge: Cambridge University Press.

Chapter 2

Appleton, J. (1975) *The Experience of Landscape,* Chichester: John Wiley.

Bennett, A.F. (1999) *Linkages in the Landscape. The Role of Corridors and Connectivity in Wildlife Conservation,* Gland & Cambridge: IUCN.

Budiansky, S. (1995) *Nature's Keepers: the New Science of Nature Management,* London: Weidenfeld & Nicolson.

Farina, A. (1998) *Principles and Methods in Landscape Ecology,* London: Chapman & Hall.

Forman, R.T.T. (1995) *Land Mosaics. The Ecology of Landscapes and Regions,* Cambridge: Cambridge University Press.

Forman, R.T.T. and Godron, M. (1986) *Landscape Ecology,* New York: Wiley.

Green, B.H. (1996) (3rd ed.) *Countryside Conservation: Landscape Ecology, Planning and Management,* London: E & FN Spon.

Grime, J.P. (1979) *Plant Strategies and Vegetation Processes,* Chichester: John Wiley.

Huston, M.A. (1994) *Biological Diversity: the Co-existence of Species on Changing Landscapes,* Cambridge: Cambridge University Press.

MacArthur, R.H. and Wilson, E.O. (1967) *The Theory of Island Biogeography,* Princeton, NJ: Princeton University Press.

Moorby, H. & Cook, H.F. (1992) 'The use of fertiliser free grass strips to protect dyke water from nitrate pollution', *Aspects of Applied Biol.* 30, 231–234.

Moore, N.W. and Hooper, M.D. (1975) 'On the Number of Bird Species in British Woods', *Biol. Conserv.* 8, 239–250.

Naveh, Z. and Lieberman, A.S. (1994) *Landscape Ecology: Theory and Application,* Berlin: Springer-Verlag.

Opdam, P. (1991) 'Metapopulation theory and habitat fragmentation: a review of holarctic breeding bird studies', *Landscape Ecology* 5, 93–106.

Pickett, S.T.A. and White, P.S. (1985) *The Ecology of Natural Disturbance and Patch Dynamics,* London: Academic Press.

Putman, R.J., Fowler, A.D. and Tout, S. (1991) 'Patterns of use of ancient grassland by cattle and horses: effects on vegetational composition and structure', *Biol. Conserv.* 56, 329–347.

Saunders, D.A. and Hobbs, R.J. (eds) (1991) *Nature Conservation (2): the Role of Corridors,* Chipping Norton, NSW: Surrey Beatty & Sons.

Sharpe, D.M. (1987) 'Vegetation dynamics in a South Wisconsin agricultural landscape'. In Turner, H.G. (ed.) *Landscape Heterogeneity and Disturbance,* New York: Springer-Verlag.

Sousa, W.P. (1984) 'The role of disturance in natural communities', *Ann. Rev. Ecol. Syst.* 15, 353–391.

Zonneveld, I.S. (1995) *Landscape Ecology,* Amsterdam: SPB Academic Publishing.

Chapter 3

Barr, C.J. and Whittaker, M. (1987) 'Trees in the British landscape–doom and boom', *Arboricultural Journal* 11, 115–126.

Barr, C.J., Bunce, R.G.H., Clarke, R.T., Fuller, R.M., Furse, M.T., Gillespie, M.K., Groom, G.B., Hallam, C.J., Hornung, M., Howard, D.C. and Ness, M.J. (1993) *Countryside Survey 1990: Main Report* (Vol. 2), London: Department of the Environment.

Benefield, C.B. and Bunce, R.G.H. (1982) *A Preliminary Visual Presentation of Land Classes in Britain,* Merlewood Research and Development Paper No. 91, Grange-over-Sands: Institute of Terrestrial Ecology.

Blankson, E.J. and Green, B.H. (1991) 'Use of landscape classification as an essential prerequisite to landscape evaluation', *Landscape and Urban Planning* 21, 149–162.

Bunce, R.G.H., Morrell, S.K. and Stel, H.E. (1975) 'The application of multivariate analysis to regional survey', *Journal of Environmental Management* 3, 151–165.

Bunce, R.G.H. and Smith, R.S. (1978) *An Ecological Survey of Cumbria,* Kendal: Cumbria County Council and Lake District Special Planning Board.

Bunce, R.G.H., Barr, C.J., Clarke, R.T., Howard, D.C. and Lane, A.M.J. (1996a) 'The ITE Merlewood Land Classification', *Journal of Biogeography* 23, 625–634.

Bunce, R.G.H., Watkins, J.W., Gillespie, M.K. and Howard, D.C. (1996b) 'The Cairngorms environment and climate change in a European context', *Botanical Journal of Scotland* 48, 127–135.

Countryside Commission (1994) *The New Map of England: A Celebration of the South-western Landscape,* Cheltenham: Countryside Commission.

Greig-Smith, P. (1964) *Quantitative Plant Ecology,* London: Butterworth.

Haines-Young, R.H., Bunce, R.G.H. and Parr, T.W. (1994) 'Countryside Information System: an information system for environmental policy development and appraisal', *Geographical Systems* 1, 329–345.

Hill, M.O. (1979) *TWINSPAN – a FORTRAN program for arranging multivariate data in an ordered two-way table by classification of the individuals and attributes,* Ithaca, New York: Section of Ecology and Systematics, Cornell University.

Hulme, M., Conway, D., Jones, P.D., Jiang, T., Barrow, E.M. and Turney, C. (1995) 'Construction of a 1961–1990 European Climatalogy for climate change modelling and impact applications', *International Journal of Climatology* 15, 1333–1363.

Jones, H.E. and Bunce, R.G.H. (1985) 'A preliminary classification of the climate of Europe from temperature and precipitation records', *Journal of Environmental Management* 20, 17–29.

Kendrew, W.G. (1953) (4th ed.) *The Climate of the Continents*, London: Oxford University Press.

Meeus, J.H.A., Wijermans, H.P. and Vroom, M.J. (1990) 'Agricultural landscapes in Europe and their transformation', *Landscape & Urban Planning* 18, 289–352.

Stanners, D. and Bourdeau, P. (1995) *Europe's Environment: the Dobris Assessment,* Copenhagen: European Environment Agency.

Watkins, J.W. and Bunce, R.G.H. (1996) 'An objective approach to landscape description'. In Aalen, F.H.A. (ed.) *Landscape Study and Management*, Dublin: Boole Press.

Wiens, J.A., Addicott, J.F., Case, T.J. and Diamond, J. (1986) 'Overview: the importance of spatial and temporal scale in ecological investigations'. In Diamond, J. and Case, T.J. (eds) *Community Ecology*, New York: Harper & Row.

Chapter 4

Beckers, A. (2000) 'Krimpenerwaard: ontwikkeling van duurzame natuur en landbouw'. In D.van Dorp *et al.* (eds) *Landschapsecologie*, Amsterdam: Boom, pp. 332–350.

Boland, D. (1994) *Hydrologisch Onderzoek Krimpenerwaard*, Landinrichtingsdienst Zuid-Holland.

De Jongh, J., de Poel, K.R., Vaessen, O. and Vos, W. (1987) *Water en Landschap in een Veenweidegebied: De Krimpenerwaard*, Utrecht: Studiecommissie Waterbeheer Natuur, Bos en Landschap.

Den Held, J.J. (1990) 'Ecologische structuur Krimpenerwaard', *Mededelingen Landinrichtingsdienst* 196.

Eggink, H.J. (1994) *Sustainable rural development in 'The Krimpenerwaard' (The Netherlands), Proceedings of the International Workshop 'Sustainable land use planning', Wageningen*, Amsterdam: Elsevier.

Heidemij Adviesbureau (1985) *Vegetatiekartering Krimpenerwaard*, Landinrichtingsdienst, Staatsbosbeheer.

Ministry of Agriculture, Nature Management and Fisheries (1990) *Nature Policy Plan of The Netherlands*, The Hague.

Moning, A. & Naberman, S. (1998) 'De waterbeheersing in de Krimpenerwaard op een nieuwe leest geschoeid', *Landinrichting* 38, 29–33.

Natuurwetenschappelijke Commissie (1986) *Herinrichting Krimpenerwaard*, Utrecht: Natuurbeschermingsraad.

PPD-Zuid-Holland (1985) *Derde Streekplanuitwerking Zuid-Holland Oost, de Krimpenerwaard,* 's-Gravenhage.

Provincie Zuid-Holland (1993) *Probleemschets Krimpenerwaard,* 's-Gravenhage.

Thijs, H.M.E. (1991) 'Bedrijfsmodellenonderzoek Krimpenerwaard', *Landinrichting* 31, 24–28.

Weidema, W.J., Goudswaard, J., Noe, C., Peeters, G.H.C. and Scheygrond, A. (1976) *Waarden van Zuid-Holland,* Rotterdam: Stichting het Zuid-Hollands Landschap.

Chapter 5

Aarseth, I. (1989) 'Fjell og fjord- stein og jord'. In Schei, N. (ed.) *Bygd og by I Norge, Sogn og Fjordane*, Gyldendal: Norsk forl., pp. 97–121.

Austad, I. (1988) 'Tree pollarding in western Norway'. In Birks, H.H., Birks, H.J., Kaland, P.E. and Moe, D. (eds) *The Cultural Landscape: Past, Present and Future,* Cambridge: Cambridge University Press, pp. 13–29.

Austad, I. and Hauge, I. (1989) 'Restoration and management of historical cultural landscapes: an important aspect of landscape ecology. Results from a cotter's farm in Laerdal, western Norway', *Landschaft und Stadt* 21, 148–157.

Austad, I. and Hauge, L. (1990) 'Juniper fields in Sogn, western Norway, a man-made vegetation type', *Nord. J. Bot.* 9, 665–683.

Austad, I. and Losvik, M.H. (1998) 'Changes in species composition following field and tree layer restoration and management in a wooded hay meadow', *Nord. J. Bot.* 18, 641–662.

Austad, I. and Skogen, A. (1990) 'Restoration of a deciduous woodland in western Norway formerly used for fodder production: effects on tree canopy and floristic composition', *Vegetatio* 88, 1–20.

Austad, I., Hauge, L. and Helle, T. (1993) *Maintenance and Conservation of the Cultural Landscape in Sogn og Fjordane, Norway*, Final report, Sogn og Fjordane College.

Austad, I., Hauge, H. and Helle, T. (1994) *Verdifulle Kulturlandskap og Kulturmarkstyper i Sogn og Fjordane*, Prioriterte Omraaider, Sogn og Fjordane College.

Austad, I., Hauge, L. and Skogen, A. (in preparation) 'Birch groves in inner Sogn, western Norway: A characteristic human-dependent vegetation type'.

Austad, I., Skogen, A., Hauge, L., Helle, T. and Timberlid, A. (1991) 'Human-influenced vegetation types and landscape elements in the cultural landscapes in inner Sogn, western Norway', *Norsk geogr. Tidsskr.* 45, 35–58.

Dahl, E., Elven, R., Moen, A. and Skogen, A. (1986) *Vegetasjonskart over Norge 1:1 500 000, Nasjonalatlas for Norge*, Statens Kartverk.

Hauge, I. (1988) 'Galdane, Laerdal, western Norway. Management and restoration of the cultural landscape'. In Birks, H.H., Birks, H.J., Kaland, P.E. and Moe, D. (eds) *The Cultural Landscape: Past, Present and Future*, Cambridge: Cambridge University Press, pp. 31–45.

Hauge, L. (1998) 'Restoration and management of a birch grove in inner Sogn formerly used for fodder production', *Norsk geogr. Tidsskr.* 52, 65–78.

Klakegg, O., Nordahl-Olsen, T., Sonstegaard, E. and Aa, A.R. (1989) *Sogn og Fjordane fylke, kvartaergeologisk kart – 1:250 000*, Norges Geologiske Undersokelse.

Kvale, A. (1980) 'Fjellgrunnen'. In Schei, N. (ed.) *Bygd og by i Norge, Sogn og Fjordane*, Gyldendal: Norsk forl., pp. 76–96.

Moe, B. and Botnen, A. (1997) 'A quantitative study of the epiphytic vegetation on pollarded trunks of *Fraxinus excelsior* at Havrå, Osterøy, western Norway', *Plant Ecology* 129, 157–177.

Chapter 6

Fielding, X. (1953) *The Stronghold*, London: Secker and Warburg.

Spratt, T.A.B. (1851) *Travels and Researches in Crete* Vol. 2, p. 276.

Chapter 7

Daskalakis, E. Dim., Director, (1987) *The Samaria Gorge: Paradise of Crete*. A publication of the Pancretan Tourist Guide *Crete All Year Round*.

Grove, A.T., Ispikoudis, I., Kazaklis, A., Moody, J.A., Papanastasis, V. and Rackham, O. (1993) *Threatened Mediterranean Landscapes: West Crete, Final Report*.

Chapter 8

Beni, C. (1889, 1958–2nd ed., 1983–3rd ed.) *Guida del Casentino,* Firenze: Nardini Editore.

Gabbrielli, A. and Settesoldi, E. (1977) *La Storia della Foreste Casentinese nelle Carte dell'Archivio dell'Opera del Duomo di Firenze, dal Secolo XIVo al XIXo,* Roma: Collano Verde 43.

Galligani, U. (1971) 'Paleosuoli e terrazzi fluviali in Casentino', *Mem. Soc. Geol. It.* 10, 247–256.

Immagini del Casentino: Lo Spirito di Una Valle (1988), Firenze: Fratelli, Minafl.

Lusini, V. (1969) *Le Sistemazioni Idraulico-forestali nei Bacini Montani del Casentino,* Tesi di laurea, Uni.Firenze.

Norcini, F.L. (1984) *Casentino Addio,* Cortona: Calosci.

Padula, M. (1983) *Storia delle foreste domaniali Casentinesi nell'Appennino Tosco-Romagnolo,* Roma: Collana Verde 63.

Pontecorvo. G. (1936) *Le Condizioni dell'Economia Rurale nell'Appennino Toscano.* II. Pratomagno e Appennini Casentinese, Firenze: R. Acc.dei Georg.

Vos, W. and Stortelder, A.H.F. (1992) (2nd ed.) *Vanishing Tuscan Landscapes. Landscape Ecology of a Submediterranean-Montane area (Solano Basin, Tuscany, Italy),* Wageningen: PUDOC.

Zangheri, P. (1966) 'Flora e vegetazione del medio ed alto Appennini Romagnolo', *Webbia* 21, 1–50.

Chapter 9

Anderson, M.A. (1980) 'The Proposed High Weald Area of Outstanding Natural Beauty: the use of landscape appraisal in the definition of its boundaries', *Landscape Research* 6, 6–10.

Brandon, P. and Short, B. (1990) *The South East from AD 1000,* London: Longman.

Countryside Commission (1994) *The High Weald: Exploring the Landscape of the Area of Outstanding Natural Beauty,* Cheltenham: Countryside Commission.

East Sussex County Council (1978) *High Weald Proposed Area of Outstanding Natural Beauty: Statement of Intent,* Lewes: East Sussex County Council.

English Nature (1997) *High Weald Natural Area Profile,* Lewes: English Nature.

FRCA (1998) *Agricultural Census Data for the High Weald AONB 1986–1996.* Report produced on behalf of the Ministry of Agriculture, Fisheries and Food by the Farming and Rural Conservation Agency (FRCA).

High Weald Forum (1995) *High Weald AONB Management Plan,* Lewes.

Land Use Consultants (1998) *The High Weald AONB: a Case for Integrated Rural Support.* Report produced by Land Use Consultants for the High Weald Unit.

Whittow, J. (1992) *Geology and Scenery in Britain,* London: Chapman & Hall.

Chapter 10

Appleton, J. (1975) *The Experience of Landscape*, Chichester: John Wiley.

Blankson, E. J. and Green, B.H. (1991) 'Use of landscape classification as an essential prerequisite to landscape evaluation', *Landscape and Urban Planning* 21, 149–162.

Bunce, R.G.H., Howard, D.C., Hallam, C.J. and Benefield, C.B. (1993) *Ecological Consequences of Land-use Change: Countryside 1990*, Vol.1, London: Department of the Environment.

Campbell, L.H. and Cooke, A.S. (eds) (1997) *The Indirect Effects of Pesticides on Farmland Birds*, London: JNCC.

Countryside Commission (1993) *Landscape Assessment Guide*, DDP423, Cheltenham.

Cook, K., Mooney, P., Hall, K., Healey, M., Watts, D. and Schreier, H. (1992) *An Evaluation of Environmentally Sensitive Areas in the Township of Langley*, Westwater Research Centre, University of British Columbia.

EDI and BUWAL (Eidgenössisches Departement des Innern, Bundesamt für Umwelt, Wald und Landschaft) (1991) *Inventar der Moorlandschaften von besonderer Schönheit und von nationaler Bedeutung*, Bern.

Fines, K.D. (1968) 'Landscape evaluation: a research project in East Sussex', *Reg. Stud.* 2, 41–55.

Green, B.H. (1993). Towards a more sustainable agriculture: time for a rural land-use strategy? *Biologist* 40, 81–85.

Green, B.H. (1999) (3rd ed.) *Countryside Conservation*, London: E & FN Spon.

Gulinck, H. and Múgica, P. (2000) 'Landscape values and threats'. In Wascher, D.M. (ed.) *European Landscapes: Classification, Evaluation and Conservation*, Copenhagen: European Environment Agency.

Hunzinger, M. (1995) 'The spontaneous reafforestation in abandoned agricultural lands: perception and aesthetic assessment by locals and tourists', *Landscape and Urban Planning* 31, 399–410

Jedicke, E. (1994) (2nd ed.) *Biotopverbund*, Stuttgart: Ulmer.

Kaule, G. (1968) *Arten-und Biotopschutz*, UTB Grosse Reihe, Stuttgart: Ulmer.

Linton, D.L. (1968) 'The assessment of scenery as a natural resource', *Scottish Geog. Mag.* 84, 219–238.

McHarg, I.L. (1969) *Design with Nature*, New York: Doubleday/Natural History Press.

Meeus, J.H.A., Wijermans, M.P. and Vroom, M.J. (1990) 'Agricultural landscapes in Europe and their transformation', *Landscape and Urban Planning* 18, 289–352.

Neef, E. (1967) *Die Theoretischen Grundlagen der Landschaftslehre*, Gotha/Leipzig: Haak.

O'Riordan, T., Wood, C. and Sheldrake, A. (1993) 'Landscapes for tomorrow', *J. Environ. Planning* 36, 123–147.

Plachter, H. (1995) 'Functional criteria for the assessment of cultural landscapes'. In Droste, B., Plachter, H. and Rossler, M. (eds) *Cultural Landscapes of Universal Value*, Jena: Fischer.

Schmithüsen, J. (1963) 'Der wissenschaftliche Landschaftsbegriff', *Mitt. Der floristisch-speziologischen Arbeitsgemeinschaft* NF 10, 9–19.

Spellerberg, I.F. (1992) *Evaluation and Assessment for Conservation*, London: Chapman & Hall.

Taylor, J.G., Zube, E.H. and Sell, L.S. (1987) 'Landscape assessment and perception research methods'. In Bechtel *et al.* (eds) *Methods in Environmetal and Behavioural Research*, New York: Van Nostrand Reinhold.

Troll, C. (1950) 'Die geographische Landschaft und ihre Forschung', *Studium Generale* 3, 163–81, Berlin: Springer-Verlag.

Usher, M.B. (1986) *Wildlife Conservation Evaluation*, London: Chapman & Hall.

Wascher, D.M., Piorr, H.P. and Kreisel-Fonck, A. (1998), 'Agricultural landscape'. In *OECD Workshop on Agri-environmental Indicators*, COM/AGR/ENV/EPOC (98) 81.

Chapter 11

CEC (1998) *Agenda 2000 – For a Stronger and Wider Union*, Communication of the Commission, DOC 97/6, Strasbourg, 90 pp.

Council of Europe (1995) *Pan-European Biological and Landscape Diversity Strategy – a Vision for Europe's Natural Heritage*, Council of Europe, UNEP, European Centre for Nature Conservation, Amsterdam, 50 pp.

Council of Europe (1997) *The Preliminary Draft European Landscape Convention*, Congress of Local and Regional Authorities of Europe, Fourth Session (Strasbourg, 3–5 June 1997), CG (4) 6 Part II, 83 pp.

Gulinck, H. and Múgica, P. (2000) 'Landscape values and threats'. In Wascher, D.M. (ed.) *European Landscapes: Classification, Evaluation and Conservation*, Copenhagen: European Environment Agency.

IUCN (1990) *United Nations List of National Parks and Protected Areas*, Gland, Switzerland: IUCN.

Jongman, R. (2000) 'Landscape classification'. In Wascher, D.M. (ed.) *European Landscapes: Classification, Evaluation and Conservation*, Copenhagen: European Environment Agency.

Klijn, J.A., Bethe, F., Wijermans, M. & Ypma, K.W. (1999) *Landscape Assessment Method at a European Level*, Report in Implementation of Action Theme 4 of PEBLDS, Tilburg and Wageningen: European Centre for Nature Conservation and Alterra – Green World Research.

Lucas, P.H.C. (1992) *Protected Landscapes: A Guide for Policy-makers and Planners*, London: Chapman & Hall.

Prieur, M. (1997) 'The law applicable to landscape in comparative and international law'. In Council of Europe Report on Preliminary Draft European Landscape Convention, CG(4) 6, Strasbourg, pp. 31–33.

Stanners, D. and Bourdeau, P. (eds) (1995) *Europe's Environment: The Dobris Assessment*, Copenhagen: European Environment Agency.

UNESCO (1995) *Operational Guidelines for the Implementation of the World Heritage Convention*, Paris.

Vervloet, J. (2000) *Pan-European Landscape Map: The Physical Geographic Map of Europe: Theoretical Backgrounds and Regional Description*. First Phase of a Project Implementation in the Framework of Action Theme 4 of PEBLDS. Wageningen: Alterra – Green World Research.

Wascher, D.M. (1995) 'Landscape Protection Areas of Europe'. In Stanners, D. and Bourdeau, P. (eds) *Europe's Environment: the Dobris Assessment*, Copenhagen: European Environment Agency.

Wascher, D.M. (1999) 'Establishing targets to assess agricultural impacts on European landscapes'. In Brouwer, F. and Crabtree, B. (eds) (1999) *Environmental Indicators and Agricultural Policy,* Project Report from a Concerted Action AIR3 – 1164 Policy measures to Control Environmental Impacts from Agriculture, Oxford: CABI Publishing, pp. 73–87.

Wascher, D.M. (ed.) (2000) European Landscapes: *Classification, Evaluation and Conservation*, Copenhagen: European Environment Agency.

Chapter 12

Baldock, D., Beaufoy, G., Brouwer, F. and Godeschalk, F. (1996) *Farming at the Margins: Abandonment or Redeployment of Agricultural Land in Europe*, London and The Hague: IEEP and LEI-DLO.

Bethe, F. and Bolsius, E.C.A. (eds) (1995) *Marginalisation of Agricultural Land in Europe – Essays and Country Studies*, The Hague: Ministry of Housing, Spatial Planning and the Environment.

Bignal, E.M. and McCracken, D.I. (1996) 'Low intensity farming systems in the conservation of the countryside', *Journal of Applied Ecology* 33, 413–424.

CEC (1988) *The Future of Rural Society*, Brussels: Com (88) 501 final.

CEC (1993) 'Support for farms in mountain, hill and less-favoured areas', *Green Europe* 2/93, Brussels.

De Putter, J. (1995) *The Greening of Europe's Agricultural Policy – the 'Agri-environmental Regulation' of the MacSharry Reform*, The Hague: Ministry of Agriculture, Nature Management and Fisheries.

Dyson, T. (1996) *Population and Food. Global Trends and Future Prospects*, London: Routledge.

Green, B.H. (2000) 'Farming the environment – lessons from New Zealand', *Town and Country Planning*, 69, 253–255.

Harvey, G. (1997) *The Killing of the Countryside*, London: Cape.

Harms, B.H., Knappen, J.P. and Rademakers, J.G. (1993) 'Landscape planning for nature restoration: comparing regional scenarios'. In Vos, C.C. and Opdam, P. (eds) *Landscape Ecology of a Stressed Environment*, London: Chapman & Hall.

NSCGP (1992) *Ground for Choices: Four Perspectives for the Rural Areas in the European Community*, The Hague: Netherlands Scientific Council for Government Policy.

O'Riordan, T., Wood, C. and Sheldrake, A. (1993) 'Landscapes for tomorrow', *Journal of Environmental Planning* 36, 123–124.

Poole, A., Pienkowski, M., McCracken, D.I., Petretti, F., Brédy, C. and Deffeyes, C. (eds) (1998) *Mountain Livestock Farming and EU Policy Development*, Proceedings of the Fifth European Forum on Nature Conservation and Pastoralism, 18–21 September 1996, Cogne, Valle d'Aosta, Italy.

Potter, C. and Lobley, M. (1992) 'The conservation status and potential of elderly farmers; results from a survey in England and Wales', *J. Rural Studies* 8, 133–43.

Stephenson, G. (1997) 'Is there life after subsidies? The New Zealand experience', *Ecos* 18, 22–26.

Vos, W., Austad, I. and Pinto Correia, T. (1994) 'Sustainable forestry in old cultural landscapes in Europe'. In Koch, N.E. (ed.) *The Scientific Basis for Sustainable Multiple-use Foresty in the European Community*, Proceedings of EU Workshop, 28–29 June 1993, Brussels, pp. 81–96.

Vos, W. and Stortelder, A.H.F. (1992) *Vanishing Tuscan Landscapes*, Wageningen: PUDOC.

Vos, W., Douw, L., Hoogendoorn, J., Korevaar, H., Pedroli, B. and Spoelstra, S.F. (1998) *Multifunctionele Landbouw – Nieuwe Wegen in het Onderzoek*, Wageningen: DLO.

Index

0646 104